GET
RICH
Vlogging

idea
Library Learning Information

Zoe Griffin

GET RICH Vlogging

Zoella did it. Alfie did it.
Now you can do it

JOHN BLAKE

John Blake Publishing Ltd

3 Bramber Court, 2 Bramber Road

London W14 9PB, England

www.johnblake

www.facebook.com/johnblakebooks

twitter.com/jblakebooks

First published in paperback in 2016

ISBN: 978 1 78606 110 2

British Library Cataloguing-in-Publication Data:

A catalogue record for this book is available from the British Library.
Design by www.envydesign.co.uk

Printed in Great Britain by CPI Group (UK) Ltd

1 3 5 7 9 10 8 6 4 2

Papers used by John Blake Publishing are natural, recyclable products made from wood grown in sustainable forests. The manufacturing processes conform to the environmental regulations of the country of origin.

Every attempt has been made to contact the relevant copyright-holders, but some were unobtainable. We would be grateful if the appropriate people could contact us.

CONTENTS

INTRODUCTION

How much do you know about the vlogging business? Before we can aspire to get rich in a certain field, we must be sure we know everything about that industry. Who are the superstars already operating in the arena? How are their vlogs different from the amateur vlogger struggling to grow traffic?

I've worked with vloggers for seven years, and I have seen first-hand how the industry has changed. In 2009, there wasn't much difference between bloggers and vloggers except for the way we presented our thoughts and insights into daily life. Initially, I chose blogging; I set up my blog LiveLikeaVIP.com in 2009 after growing disillusioned with my job writing for a national newspaper. I was the showbiz gossip column editor of the *Sunday Mirror*, but nobody my age bought or read a newspaper and it made me think there was a market for online content aimed at teens and twenty-somethings. I chose blogging over vlogging because I loved writing, and I knew how to work with photos after watching busy newspaper departments find the right images to accompany stories. Had I decided to make video content back in 2009, life would have been very different.

While I was busy writing about celebrities I'd interviewed, and taking photos to show how their outfits could be copied with cheaper alternatives, people like Zoella and Fleur De Force were sitting in their bedrooms talking to camera about what they'd been up to and where they'd been shopping. Instead of photographing their clothes, they'd make 'haul' videos in which they tipped open the contents of their shopping bags and held the items up to the camera. Both blogging and vlogging were ways of reaching a new generation of content consumers: blogging in 2D, and vlogging in 3D.

Fashion retailers were – and still are – desperately keen to get involved with these new media, inviting bloggers and vloggers to events and parties showcasing their products. In the early days, bloggers and vloggers were treated as one, and we'd regularly meet up in the penthouses of London's most exclusive five-star hotels, such as Sanderson and The May Fair, for drinks or afternoon tea, while a fashion brand laid on a presentation for us. Sometimes, there could be as many as three or four events a week, as more and more retailers realised the power of online content. I found myself socialising with bloggers and vloggers more often than I did with my old group of friends. Since blogging and vlogging had brought us together, they were often the topics of conversation when we met up. We'd ask questions like: were we being efficient with our time? What were we doing to grow traffic and subscribers? What tools had we found to make blogging and vlogging easier?

In late 2012 to early 2013, I noticed things starting to change. When some vloggers reached six to seven figures in their subscriber numbers, retailers shifted their approach. Vloggers and bloggers were no longer invited to the same events, and started being treated differently. The number of events decreased as marketing managers followed the numbers: they were able to see how much influence vloggers had by looking at the number of subscribers to their YouTube channels and views of their videos. As a result, PR agencies could be more focused and aim for mentions on the vlogs with the biggest audiences. Hosting events can never guarantee coverage, as a vlogger's attendance at the event does not oblige them to talk about it. Therefore, the events were cut back and the budget was spent paying for sponsored content on the vlogs and blogs with the most influence.

By 2013, several vloggers had turned their hobby into a business, as sponsored content and YouTube advertising rates meant they could earn more from their vlog than they could from more traditional jobs. Fortunately, blogging caught up as PR agencies used social media statistics to see which bloggers had the most reach. We'd be approached by a PR rep or a brand manager via email, negotiate a fee and then post our content. Socialising had to be cut back as we were all engrossed in posting and promoting our work. I didn't want to turn anything down as it was an exciting time and I was constantly busy. However, I still found time to catch up with the blogs and vlogs my friends created, and I noticed the vloggers had similar levels of sponsored content to me.

Vloggers with high traffic levels signed up to the agency Gleam Futures to maximise their earning potential, and I signed up to Mode Media (formerly known as Glam), which takes on bloggers as well as vloggers. In Chapter 6 I'll explain how both of these agencies can help anyone wanting to 'get rich vlogging', and how they should be approached. There is little doubt that having these big professional companies on board to negotiate deals has helped vlogging to be seen as a legitimate industry and not just a pastime.

Although I didn't start vlogging in the early days of YouTube, I witnessed those who did and I watched how they grew traffic. I noticed there were tactics they applied that aspiring vloggers didn't think about using. These traits set successful vloggers apart from those who failed to grow their subscriber numbers. I explore a different trait in each chapter of this book, looking at what the most famous vloggers have in common when it comes to thinking of a theme for their vlogs, growing social media numbers and monetising their vlogs through several revenue streams.

As I am primarily a blogger rather than a vlogger, I can be more open. I have nothing to hide because it won't hinder my business if the readers of this book all become famous and rich on a global level. Some YouTubers are reluctant to share the secrets of their success because they don't want you to enter the industry and compete with them for work. I want you to do well so I can watch some fresh, entertaining videos, and so I can be proved right – it's not too late for anyone to start vlogging and making money from it, as long as you're prepared to work hard and you have a passion for your topic.

Once you have the passion and motivation, you're ready to get started, and this book will help you to do it in an organised fashion so you don't waste time or energy. Without a clear sense of direction, it's easy to be swallowed up by the noise of YouTube. More than 300 hours of video are uploaded to YouTube every minute, so you need to be different if you want to be successful. Most videos receive fewer than 1,000 views and, if you want to surpass that figure, you need a solid plan.

My plan has been formulated through contact with and observation of the following vloggers:

- AmazingPhil by Phil Lester (youtube.com/AmazingPhil) – 3.4 million subscribers
- Caspar Lee (youtube.com/dicasp) – 5.9 million subscribers
- Catrific by Cat Valdes (youtube.com/catrific) – 730,000 subscribers
- Charlieissocoollike by Charlie McDonnell (youtube.com/charlieissocoollike) – 2.4 million subscribers
- Danisnotonfire by Dan Howell (youtube.com/danisnotonfire) – 5.6 million subscribers
- Estée Lalonde (youtube.com/essiebutton) – 1.1 million subscribers
- Fleur De Force (youtube.com/FleurDeForce) – 1.4 million subscribers
- JacksGap by Jack and Finn Harries (youtube.com/JacksGap) – 4.2 million subscribers

- Jenna Marbles (youtube.com/JennaMarbles) – 15.9 million subscribers
- Jim Chapman (youtube.com/jimchapman) – 2.5 million subscribers
- Joey Graceffa (youtube.com/joeygraceffa) – 6 million subscribers
- KSI (youtube.com/KSI) – 12.8 million subscribers
- iJustine (youtube.com/ijustine) – 2.8 million subscribers
- Marcus Butler (youtube.com/MarcusButler) – 4.3 million subscribers
- Michelle Phan (youtube.com/MichellePhan) – 8.4 million subscribers
- Niomi Smart (youtube.com/niomismart) – 1.6 million subscribers
- PewDiePie (youtube.com/PewDiePie) – 44 million subscribers
- PointlessBlog by Alfie Deyes (youtube.com/PointlessBlog) – 5 million subscribers
- Sprinkle of Glitter by Louise Pentland (youtube.com/Sprinkleofglitter) – 2.4 million subscribers
- IISuperwomanII by Lilly Singh (youtube.com/IISuperwomanII) – 8.6 million subscribers
- Tanya Burr (youtube.com/tanyaburr) – 3.4 million subscribers
- ThatcherJoe by Joe Sugg (youtube.com/ThatcherJoe) – 6.6 million subscribers
- Troye Sivan (youtube.com/TroyeSivan) – 4 million subscribers
- Tyler Oakley (youtube.com/tyleroakley) – 8 million subscribers
- Zoella by Zoe Sugg (youtube.com/zoella) – 10.2 million subscribers

Looking at the list above may make you feel intimidated. The concept of reaching a million subscribers or more may seem daunting as you stand at the start of your vlogging journey, but none of the vloggers above reached a million followers overnight. They all started with one or two subscribers and then added a few more.

If you'd seriously like to 'get rich vlogging', then I urge you to put the fear of failure to the back of your mind and start in a methodical way, growing your vlog step by step as outlined in the chapters of this book. What have you got to lose?

CHAPTER 1

GETTING STARTED

The dictionary definition of a vlog is 'a video journal that is uploaded to the Internet, or a blog in which the postings are primarily videos'. With this general definition, many people mistakenly rush into vlogging thinking all they need to get started is a video camera and access to the Internet.

If it were that simple, why is it that some vloggers receive hundreds of thousands or millions of views, while others struggle to reach over a hundred? The answer is that the well-known vloggers have a constant theme that runs throughout their videos, and this is often lacking in amateur vloggers' work. Let's take two professional vloggers – Tanya Burr and Marcus Butler. Tanya's YouTube channel contains a high proportion of beauty videos. She regularly posts make-up tutorials, and talks about grooming products she has bought and she recommends. Viewers have

1

reason to watch the videos because they are being educated: they are learning how to apply make-up better. Marcus, on the other hand, is more of a comedian, regularly uploading videos of pranks he's carried out. Viewers are entertained; they are having a break from the humdrum of their daily lives and laughing out loud at something silly.

Successful vloggers either educate or entertain – or both – by picking a theme that runs throughout their videos. They often post about their daily life in addition to this educational or entertaining content, but these daily uploads usually reference the subject they cover in their other vlogs. When you visit your favourite vlogger's YouTube channel, you know exactly what types of videos you will see, unlike when you visit the channel of a vlogger who is just starting out and hasn't paid adequate attention to why they're vlogging or what their long-term goals are. Themes keep viewers coming back to a vlogger's channel, as people like to watch the development of a storyline, laugh at the prank that has been talked about in a previous video or see the next instalment of a complicated make-up tutorial.

Themes that work well on vlog channels include computer gaming, agony aunt advice, fashion and style talk, make-up tutorials, cookery demonstrations, comedy, top-ten lists and random short features. However, before you make a decision on what direction you'd like to go in, it's vital to answer the following questions:

WHAT INTERESTS YOU MORE THAN ANYTHING ELSE?

It's very tempting to model yourself on the most famous vloggers. Zoe 'Zoella' Sugg has 10 million subscribers, so if you copy what she does exactly will you get 10 million subscribers too? It wouldn't be hard to follow a similar model. You could make vlogs about baking, shopping and mental health, and you could talk in a super-positive tone of voice. You could go further and buy some pets so you can copy her relationship with her guinea pigs Percy and Pippin. But you wouldn't get 10 million subscribers that way. You'd struggle to get ten. It would be obvious to anyone who watches Zoe's videos that you were trying to copy her, and nobody wants to tune into a copycat when they can watch the real thing.

Ignore other vloggers, and give some thought to the topics you enjoy talking and learning about. This is important for two reasons. Firstly, you'll struggle to come across as educational or entertaining if you're not interested in the subject yourself. If you're simply trying to copy another vlogger, it will be reflected in the quality of your content. Successful vloggers have a special ability to connect with their audience and to give of themselves without holding back, and that only happens if you believe what you're talking about in your videos. Vloggers who fake an interest will appear untrustworthy and unlikeable, and viewers will switch off midway through their videos, never to return, let alone subscribe. Secondly, a successful vlog requires at least as much work as a full-time job. The more hours you put in, the more chance you have of growing an audience. You'll find it difficult to motivate yourself to spend hours creating and publicising something you don't care about.

For example, consider a typical day at work. If your boss gives you a dull task like sweeping the floor or cleaning the toilet, you're likely to procrastinate. When it's time to do the task, you'll probably do the bare minimum and the expression on your face will show what you really think of the work you're doing. You cannot perform your best work when you're not passionate about the job in hand. Because of the hours of work that go into making, editing and sharing vlogs, picking a theme that you're only moderately interested in would be the equivalent of being told to clean the toilet twenty times a day.

Britain's most popular vlogger KSI says he achieved 12 million subscribers only because he had a genuine love for playing computer games and making videos. 'To be successful you have to be passionate. You have to be extremely passionate about your art,' he said in BBC documentary *The Rise of the Superstar Vloggers*. 'Every video I've done, I've crafted it to the way I've wanted it to be. I've wanted my videos to be entertaining and for people to laugh at certain points, and it makes me happy if I make people happy. If you don't love what you do, then stop!

'A lot of people think YouTube is quite easy, and it isn't. I've been doing it for six or seven years now and I'd say the hardest time was the first three or four years. You're constantly making new videos and you're constantly putting up content. I work every single day to expand my brand.'

TIP: YOU NEED TO BE MORE PASSIONATE ABOUT YOUR SUBJECT THAN YOU ARE ABOUT SLEEP!

Men's fashion and grooming vlogger Robin James (youtube. com/TheUtterGutter) has 65,000 YouTube subscribers and is growing his channel in addition to holding down a full-time job. He works Monday to Friday, then spends Saturday filming videos and Sunday editing them.

He says: 'I don't often see my friends that much, but I love vlogging and I'm enjoying what I do. That's why I'm happy to make sacrifices to grow my YouTube channel. I want to be successful and make informative videos, and, if fame is a result of that, then great.'

Robin says he is prepared to sacrifice sleep if it means he can create more content. He genuinely enjoys talking about clothes and male grooming products, and said he would stop and spend his weekends seeing friends and relaxing if he didn't enjoy it.

Fashion and music vlogger Helen Anderson (youtube. com/snakebitesparkles) agrees. She adds: 'It's been four years of hard work to get traffic to my vlog. People come up to me in the street and say they think I lead a perfect life, but they don't see all the work and stress and arguments that being a YouTuber can cause. I can be working until really, really late at night at times to make sure I have an upload.'

Picking the right theme may involve hours of soul-searching, which is not always a pleasant task, but there are ways to make the process easier. Grab a pen and a sheet of A4 paper, and divide the sheet into two columns. On the left-hand side, make a list of things that interest you. Now ask yourself: what subjects could you talk about for twenty-four hours a day? Circle those and cross everything else off the list. On the right-hand side, make a list of your skill sets. Are you a great researcher? Do you have high energy levels and a great deal of enthusiasm? Or do you have a dry, witty sense of humour and a love of satire? Ask others to help you with your list, as sometimes people see qualities in you that you never realised you had.

At the end of this task, your paper should show one or two subjects on the left and a longer list of skills on the right. A way you can be unique and offer something interesting to the vlogging community is by covering the topics on the left-hand side and presenting your videos in a format that fits in with the skill sets you've listed on the right-hand side. You might end up with an idea to cover beauty in a humorous way or feature gaming in a more energetic way than other gaming vloggers.

Don't be afraid if you have diverse interests. For example, maybe you are interested in sport and beauty? This could make for a pretty interesting vlog. While there are lots of fitness vlogs and lots of beauty vlogs, there aren't so many that combine beauty and sport, telling us cute but practical hairstyles for the gym or how to protect our skin from sweating. Try it, and you can always switch things up later if you discover that you enjoy the beauty part more than the sports part or vice versa.

Once you have picked your theme with the help of your lists, the final step is to do some research. Go to YouTube and enter the subjects from the left-hand column into the search box. Which vloggers are already operating in your area? Are there any you particularly admire? If so, subscribe to them – you want to keep tabs on what they're doing, and perhaps there will be an opportunity to collaborate in the future. Are there any vloggers in that subject area who aren't hitting high traffic figures? What can you offer that they can't? What mistakes are they making?

Turn over the sheet on which you wrote your original list of subjects and skill sets. Divide the blank side into two equal columns, and write 'Do' at the top of one and 'Don't' on the other. Under 'Do', list the vloggers you admire and explain what it is you like about them. Under 'Don't', list some vloggers you aren't keen on and explain what they're doing wrong.

Store this piece of paper in a place where you can access it regularly. You should look at it at least once a week to stay focused and avoid going off message. Reviewing it will also keep you motivated as you'll be reminding yourself that you have a unique place in the vlogging industry and that you have the skills to achieve success.

TIP: REVIEW YOUR FORMAT BASED ON VIEWERS' FEEDBACK

Twins Niki and Sammy have almost 200,000 YouTube subscribers to their vlog NikiNSammy (youtube.com/nikinsammy). Their advice is: 'It takes a while for each of us to develop our voice as a brand but, once you have that, you can change some elements while keeping the core the same.

'We try different formats on our channel to keep it fresh and topical – from reactions to collaborations. But we're still us. We're constantly thinking, "Are we enjoying this?" and "Are they – the viewers – enjoying this?" What we do is not set in stone. It's more organic and I think that's what helps people to relate to it.'

WHO WILL BE YOUR AUDIENCE?

YouTube has 1 billion active viewers per month. Some of them will be interested in what you have to say, some will hate you and some will be indifferent. You can't please everyone.

To be successful, you need to close your mind to negativity and focus on what you can control. With a little thought and research it's possible to identify groups who are interested in your topic. If you learn as much as you can about the people in these groups, you will not only attract them, but you will remain relevant to them.

Beatles star John Lennon once said: 'Trying to please everybody is impossible. If you did that, you'd end up in the middle with nobody liking you. You've just got to make the decision about what you think is your best, and do it.' The Beatles went on to sell 65 million albums worldwide to a generation of music fans. They found a sound that was unique to them, stuck with it and the fans loved it.

John Lennon's advice applies to vlogging as well as music. There is no point making videos containing lots of different elements in an attempt to keep every single one of the world's billion YouTube users happy. Trying to make people interested in what you have to say takes time and energy, and means you're not doing as much as you can to please the people who are already interested in your subject. The way to grow viewers and subscribers is to work out who your audience is and what their expectations are, then consistently deliver content that you know this group of people will like.

Music manager Scooter Braun discovered Justin Bieber on

YouTube in 2008 and liked what he saw so much that he persuaded Justin and his mother to move to Atlanta so he could manage Justin's career. After signing him up to Island Def Jam, Scooter made Justin create more YouTube videos to grow an audience so his records would sell. He succeeded – Justin's debut album *My World* was certified platinum in the US in 2009, and he became the first artist to have seven songs from his debut album chart on the Billboard Hot 100. How did they do it? At the 2016 Consumer Electronics Show (CES) conference keynote speech, Scooter said: 'My career started sat on the sofa in my underpants, thinking of ways I could get more people to watch my videos. Then it clicked – I needed to keep it simple. If you want to make YouTube work for you, don't make content for billions of people. Don't try and think of the broad spectrum you could reach and aim for people sitting on the fence. Look at yourself. If you feel something, there's a good chance some other people will feel the same way. Go to your office or bedroom, say what you're interested in and how it makes you feel.'

Only when you are clear in your mind as to the subject you want to vlog about should you start to think of your audience. By this, I mean working out which groups of people are interested in the same subject as you, and thinking about their personality traits and other interests. But why should you think of your audience at all? The answer is because you'll be talking to them when you're looking down the camera, and you need to know how to address them. You need to treat your viewers as friends and forge a connection with them, and you can't do that if you don't know anything about what these people are like.

It may be a good idea to grab another sheet of paper and a pen, and answer these questions:

HOW OLD ARE THESE PEOPLE?

It's important to know how old your audience is so you can talk to them in an appropriate tone. If your viewers are older and looking for factual information, they won't appreciate a quirky, jokey tone as much as a teenager would.

Many of the vlogging superstars that I've met and featured in this book have audiences under thirty years old on average. However, if you want to appeal to an older market, you can still be successful. All you need is an awareness of how formal or informal you need to be. The vloggers featured in this book are successful because they've adapted their tone to suit their audience, not because teenagers are more active on YouTube. In fact, YouTube CEO Susan Wojcicki claims YouTube now reaches more users in the 18–49-year-old demographic than any other TV network. It is possible to attract older viewers, as long as you don't annoy them by talking down to them.

WHAT LEVEL OF EDUCATION HAVE THEY REACHED?

You're in a tricky situation here. You don't want to look shallow and superficial, but you also don't want to make others feel stupid by referring to things they haven't been taught. Knowing their level of education will help you realise how much technical knowledge you can assume in your videos, and it will also help you decide how much of your own educational background to share.

You may have noticed that some of the successful vloggers in the UK act a lot younger than they are. Tanya Burr and Zoe Sugg are in their mid-twenties, but they are still able to connect with teenage girls. This is because they don't talk about graduation, nor do they cover subjects like drinking alcohol or clubbing, as they know some of their viewers are too young to have experienced these things.

If you can work out what your audience is going through, you'll know what to cover and what to leave out.

WHEN DO PEOPLE HAVE TIME TO WATCH YOUR VIDEOS?

It's crucial to get the length of a video right, and that largely depends on an audience. Younger viewers tend to have more free time and spend longer browsing YouTube, and as a result they are more fickle. They dip in and out of content as they are under fewer time constraints. Older viewers tend to search for an individual subject and watch one video explaining that subject in detail.

If you have a younger audience, shorter videos work best to maintain a viewer's interest. If you have an older audience, your priority is to show you're answering the viewer's need in the first minute, but there is more flexibility to talk for as long as it takes to explain the answer.

WHERE ARE THEY WATCHING THE VIDEOS?

Fifty per cent of videos are viewed on a mobile device, according to YouTube CEO Susan Wojcicki. If you think your audience is likely to use a mobile device and enjoy vlogs during their daily commute or while they're doing something else, such as watching one of the mainstream TV channels, you need to try extra hard to make your videos as attention-grabbing as possible. This is because a viewer's attention is likely to be distracted if they're multi-tasking. If the other thing they're doing excites them more than your video, they will zone out and stop watching. As the percentage of viewers watching videos on mobile devices is constantly growing, it's never been more important to keep your videos short and snappy and full of things your audience find interesting. If you lose their attention momentarily, they could turn their mobile device off and do something else.

WHAT OTHER VLOGGERS DO THEY WATCH, IF ANY?

Watching a vlog isn't like supporting a football team. Viewers can watch two or more vloggers and like them equally. See if there are any other vloggers in your field who aim at the same age group, and talk to people of your target age group to find out which vloggers they watch. Having an idea of your audience's wider viewing habits both enables you to keep an eye on the competition and to identify vloggers to collaborate with to widen your appeal.

Answering the questions above will help you determine what your audience wants, so you can meet their needs and satisfy them. Satisfied viewers will keep coming back and they are more likely to tell other people about you, helping you to grow your reach. If you arrogantly started showing off about a subject to a group of people without taking the time to ask questions or find out what they were interested in, do you think they'd like you? Of course not. You can only bond with people – and viewers – if you take the time to get to know them and find out what they like.

TIP: PUT PASSION FOR YOUR SUBJECT AND A DESIRE TO CONNECT WITH AN AUDIENCE ABOVE FINANCIAL TARGETS

Vlogger Fleur Bell has more than a million subscribers to her main channel, Fleur De Force, which she started in 2009. She made a show for Channel 4, *How to Be Internet Famous*, and her advice was: 'I think what's really important now for anyone starting a YouTube channel is not to start thinking, "I'm going to make a load of cash." At the end of the day, it doesn't work for everyone and not everyone does make a lot of money. If you're passionate about it, then that's what comes across in the content and you're more likely to make it work.

'The way to not be successful on YouTube is to do the same content as everyone else and do that because you think it's how the successful people do it. People love YouTube because everyone's unique and they're following different unique characters and personalities. You'll be followed if you can show you are unique and can be yourself.'

Choosing what to vlog about and picking a theme can be time-consuming. Don't give up! You need to start your vlogging journey on a solid footing if you're to have any chance of success. In the next chapter, I talk about how you can build a brand. You can only do that once you have picked a theme, because having a clear sense of direction will help you stay on track and focused.

After reading this chapter, you should have:

☐ Created a list of your interests
☐ Created a list of your skill sets
☐ Chosen your unique theme based on your interests and skill sets
☐ Analysed your audience
☐ Stored your lists in a safe place so you can refer to them at a
  later date

CHAPTER 2

EMBRACE YOUR INDIVIDUALITY

Now you have picked your theme, your next task is to think carefully about how you're going to draw attention to your vlog and make people aware it exists. If you look at the YouTube channels of some of your favourite vloggers, you will notice there is another thing they have in common besides being educative or entertaining: they have all thought carefully about the look and feel of their channel.

Successful vloggers make themselves into mini media networks by branding their channel in a way their audience likes. Most of them have a name for their channel that's slightly different to their real name, and all of them have a unique logo that they stamp over their videos, so the audience knows who's made them. Brand recall is the goal here. The objective behind a catchy name and logo isn't only to identify a vlogger's brand, but also to make sure that if someone sees the channel even once, then the name will be memorable. This way, people will know where to go to get more of the same content.

Successful vloggers' videos are in no way random: their brand identity runs throughout each one. Often, they use the same backdrop or setting. Sometimes they have quirky catchphrases or sayings. They rarely change their physical appearance, as their image is closely related to their brand. They'll have thought about the style of clothes they wear and their hairstyle to ensure viewers think they're cool. Fashion vloggers must be presentable and polished at all times to reflect their content, while comedy vloggers often play on a slightly unkempt, scruffy appearance so they come across as jokers. Remember that viewers have short attention spans. Sometimes they'll make up their mind about a vlogger's channel before that vlogger opens their mouth. For that reason, it's important that you dress with your audience in mind so that you keep the attention of people who have similar interests to you.

If the concept of brand identity still seems confusing, think about the BBC. If you see those three letters during the opening credits for a TV show, then it may provoke certain thoughts. We assume the BBC produces high-quality programmes. We presume there won't be any swearing or nudity before 9pm, and we expect the channel's news coverage to be trustworthy, independent and presented by smartly-dressed newsreaders. Once you've enjoyed one news bulletin or drama made by the BBC, the next time you see the BBC logo it will remind you of the show you liked and give you high expectations for the show you're about to watch.

Perhaps the next time you're channel-surfing, you'll remember that you've previously enjoyed two shows by the BBC, so you pick its channels over Channel 4 or Sky 1.

Vloggers build up their brand identity and loyalty in much the same way. Their videos consistently contain the same elements so viewers know what to expect, and they are branded with a name and a logo so viewers can find them again.

It's important to be clear on your brand identity before you start filming. Building a brand relies on consistency, and if you're unsure of your identity, it's impossible to be consistent. The basic components of building a brand include: thinking of a name, designing a logo and graphics, developing a theme tune, deciding on a personal image and picking a location. You may have some other ideas about how you can stamp your personality over your videos based on repeatedly doing something you like or are good at, but let's start by working on the basics.

NAME

A good name has three characteristics: it's catchy, it means something and it's short and to the point. Ideally, you want to think of a creative name which has multiple meanings that all relate to the content in some way. This is not easy. Don't beat yourself up if you can't think of a name that's remarkably witty and satirical. It's more important to come up with something that's unique and meaningful to you than to sit for hours and get depressed because you think another vlogger came up with a better name than you did. Question whether the other vlogger's name in itself is any good, or whether the name seems good now the vlogger's established and he or she has used it so much that it appears to fit. For example, look at the food brand Marmite. The name Marmite seems ridiculous when taken out of context but, as we use it so much, we know what it stands for and it seems to work. For this reason, there is no point worrying about a name. If you really can't think of anything, you could just use the name you were born with – it's worked for people like Marcus Butler, Joey Graceffa, Jim Chapman and Tanya Burr. Being good at thinking up a name does not mean you'll be a great vlogger.

However, I recommend spending a little time on it with a good old-fashioned brainstorming session before you give up. Ask yourself:

WHAT IS THE MAIN THEME OR SUBJECT OF MY VLOG?

As Google owns YouTube, there are many advantages to having your vlog's subject matter in its name. People will be searching for that topic on Google, and if your vlog's name includes it, there's more chance of the YouTube link to your vlog coming up in the Google search results. This is a great opportunity for new people to find out about your vlog, especially now that YouTube is such a crowded marketplace.

Write down terms related to your theme that people are likely to enter in a Google search. I suggest leaving a large gap between each word or term so you can cut up the piece of paper at the end of the exercise and rearrange all the elements to create the ideal name.

HOW ARE YOU DIFFERENT FROM OTHER VLOGGERS WHO COVER THE SAME SUBJECT?

In the last chapter, I suggested that it's still possible to make an impact in a competitive market like fashion or beauty. The way to get ahead is to use your unique skills to present your videos in a different way and incorporate elements other vloggers are missing. What are the skills and elements that are unique to you? Write them down.

DO YOU REALLY WANT TO INCLUDE YOUR FULL NAME?

It's important to think long-term. If you apply all the principles in this book and work hard, your vlog is going to take off and grow. People will forever link your name to the vlog if you name the vlog after yourself. You might often get spotted in the street, and complete strangers will call out your name.

Consider how it will affect any future career path you want to pursue if everyone automatically thinks about your vlog when they hear your name. It might work pretty well if you can imagine yourself having a career related to the subject you cover in your vlog, as your vlog could help you to establish yourself as an expert. But what if you have a comedy vlog and you see yourself with a future in politics? People won't take you seriously. This is why many vloggers use either their first name or their surname. For example, Zoe Sugg uses Zoella and her brother Joe Sugg uses ThatcherJoe. Fleur Bell uses Fleur De Force and Phil Lester uses AmazingPhil. Their fans know their real names, but there's still a degree of anonymity leaving the door open for future ventures. I know it sounds odd, but write down your name on your original piece of paper.

> ### TIP: GO ONLINE!
> If you feel silly cutting and playing with pieces of paper, then there are some genius online name-generating programmes available. Bust a Name (bustaname.com) enables you to enter the words related to your vlog and it will randomly generate different combinations of those words.

Once you have a few candidates for the name, think about your target audience. Will they find it amusing and attention-grabbing? At this point, get some feedback from your friends and people who fit into your target audience. Ask them to give you constructive feedback and suggest other ideas if they don't like your offerings. Is the name too short or too long? Having a long name could hinder you, as long names are more likely to be misspelled and tend to be harder for people to remember. Work with your feedback group – their suggestions might lead you to come up with names that are remarkably better than your first attempts.

The final step is to make sure you can own the name across the whole of the World Wide Web. There is no point in giving your vlog a name that someone else uses on social media, forcing you to use a different social media handle. Viewers will struggle to contact you, and you'll damage brand recall as people won't be hearing the name of your vlog as much. Check whether you can set up Twitter, Facebook, Snapchat and Instagram accounts in the name you like. If you can't, I'm afraid it's back to the drawing board.

You should also check whether you can buy a website domain name. Eventually, you'll be setting up a website or blog as an extra revenue stream, and you can only do this effectively if you can give the website the same name as your vlog. Your viewers will assume you are behind any website that uses your vlogging name. If that's not the case, you'll be giving the company that made the website a lot of your valuable traffic. Go to a reliable web host like GoDaddy (Godaddy.com) or Bluehost (bluehost.com), hold your breath and pray your name hasn't been taken. Otherwise, another brainstorming session is needed, I'm afraid.

LOGO AND GRAPHICS

Logos serve as visual reminders to viewers. Your logo should be powerful enough to trigger people to think about the type of vlogs you make as soon as they see it. Think of Apple's part-eaten apple, Audi's four interlinked rings or the Nike swoosh. Everyone knows the apple is associated with fancy phones and computers, the rings are a sign of a luxury car, and the swoosh signifies sports gear. A logo will give your vlog a stronger sense of brand identity.

It's worth taking the time to come up with a good logo as you'll be using it often. Your logo will appear on promotional material like business cards and posters, and you may also choose to have it as one of the profile pictures for your social media accounts. There's nothing worse than rushing a logo and then getting bored or embarrassed by it later down the line. You can't expect others to like your logo if you don't like it yourself.

When designing your logo, make sure the design sums up what your vlog is about. This is important for anyone with an online brand – bloggers and vloggers – as little visual clues are useful in helping people to remember your content. My blog Live Like a VIP has lots of stars in the design because 'star' is another term for 'VIP' in the celebrity world. Grab a thesaurus and look up words related to your vlogging theme. Do any of those words conjure up a strong visual image that you could incorporate into your logo?

Your logo will be the first thing viewers see when they visit your YouTube channel as it's positioned at the top of the page, so it's vital to make it look visually attractive. Flick through some magazines for cool images that relate to your vlog and create a mood board. You could do the same online by browsing websites and saving the images or 'pinning' them to a Pinterest Board. Hopefully, you will notice a recurring pattern or image running throughout your mood board. Focus on that type of image. Is there a way you can simplify it? YouTube doesn't offer much space for a logo to be displayed, and a complicated design may struggle when it's shrunk. Your viewers should be able to glance at your logo and understand the theme of your vlog and what image you're trying to project.

It's also a very good idea to look at other vloggers for inspiration. Don't pay too much attention to the colours and fonts they've used as you want your logo to be as unique as possible. Instead, think about how they've designed something that reflects their brand. What have they used in their logo that sums up what their videos are about? If there are no images, how have they picked a text font that indicates the type of audience they're aiming at?

With some vague ideas in mind, it's almost time to put pen

to paper. There are just four more design elements to consider – word-to-image ratio, colour, font and size.

WORD-TO-IMAGE RATIO

All logos can be divided into three types. The first is a symbol or an icon with no text, similar to the Nike swoosh or Apple's apple. As soon as you see those symbols, you know what the brand is selling. It's very hard to think of a unique symbol that will provide some brand association with your vlog, but one option would be to use your face. You could sketch your face or create a simple cartoon or caricature. Don't worry if you can't draw – childlike doodles are often hilarious. If your logo triggers an emotional reaction like a laugh, viewers are much more likely to remember it.

The second type of logo is a word or an abbreviation. Be creative with the lettering and aim for fancy fonts and colours but don't make it over-complicated. It needs to be easy to reproduce for branded material like posters and flyers.

The third – and most common – logo is a combination of a word and an icon. Using a combination of lettering and symbols, users can look at a YouTube logo and recognise the symbol, but there's a word to back it up and drive the brand association home. For example, Charlie McDonnell from charlieissocoollike (2.4 million subscribers) uses his face as the logo on his YouTube page. His face is instantly recognisable as we've seen it so many times in his videos. However, he's also written his name in simple white capital letters next to his face, to reinforce the fact that it's his channel.

COLOUR

Colours stick in people's minds. You want to create a logo in a colour that's associated with your brand, so that when people see that particular shade they think of your vlog. Think about Cadbury's chocolate and its Dairy Milk bar. It's a unique shade of purple, isn't it? Often I end up craving chocolate if I see that purple colour. What colour do you want to represent your vlog? If you have a healthy eating or eco-campaigning vlog, you may want to use a particular shade of green. Fashion and beauty vlogs look great in pink or red text to appear both bold and girly.

FONT

Think about your target audience. If you're aiming at a young, fun audience, you can be more creative and funky with your lettering. If you want to educate people with political commentary, you should look for a classic font that appears strong and professional. Above all else, make sure it's readable when it's blown up and shrunk down, so it looks good on huge banners as well as tiny profile pictures.

SIZE

YouTube recommends uploading images that are 800 by 800 px (pixels), so make sure you keep those specifications in mind when designing your logo. Don't create something massive as it may not look so good at 800 by 800 px. The small circular icon on a YouTube channel is only 98 by 98 px, so make sure you keep it simple.

TIP: SHOP AROUND FOR A PROFESSIONAL DESIGNER

There are some great-value websites that allow you to get input from a professional designer. This is particularly helpful if you know what you want and lack the skills to draw it out on paper, or if you don't know where to start and want an outside opinion to kick-start the creative process. My favourite is Fiverr (Fiverr.com). Search for 'logo design' and choose your favourite designer based on their portfolio. The basic services cost only $5! I've also used Freelancer (Freelancer.com), which has more skilled designers but tends to be slightly more expensive.

THEME TUNE

When you hear the *Eastenders* or *Neighbours* theme tunes, you know immediately what you're going to see on screen following the opening credits. You may not be anywhere near a TV, but if you hear the theme tune played on the radio or in a bar it will still cause you to think of the show and its characters and storylines. Your goal is to create a catchy tune that sticks in people's heads and makes them think of your vlog as soon as they hear it.

When it comes to music, you need to be aware of copyright. You can't just pick an obscure song from one of your favourite artists and edit it into your next video, as you'll be violating usage rights. If you're musical, you may want to create something yourself. If you're not, the easiest option is to use YouTube's audio library. This is a massive database of free music and sound effects.

You can find the audio library by logging into YouTube and

selecting the *Creator Studio* menu. Click on *Create* and you'll see a link for *Audio Library*. There you will see options for free music, ad-supported music and sound effects. Ad-supported music means that ads will play before your video when you use one of these songs, and the ad revenue will be given to the artist who made the track. In general, it's not a good idea to choose ad-supported music, as you want to monetise your videos with your own ads.

It's best to make use of YouTube's free music when making a theme tune, but be aware that you can't always use it without any attribution. If you see a circular symbol with a person standing in it to the left of the popularity bar and the download link, you need to make sure you mention the author of the song somewhere in the video or the description box when you upload the vlog to YouTube. Usually, there will be a full description of what attribution you need to give when you click on the song file's name.

Take your time picking a piece of music. If you settle for the first thing you hear, you may be missing something better. YouTube's audio library is vast, so have fun exploring it. Just make sure you keep a list so you can easily go back to songs you like. Ask friends and your target market for feedback once you've made a shortlist. After all, they're going to be listening to it a lot when your vlogging career takes off and you start to make several videos a week.

PERSONAL IMAGE

One of the best things about vlogging is being free to reinvent yourself. Zoella has talked many times about how she was shy at school and suffered from crippling anxiety, but talking to the camera helped her build confidence. The on-screen Zoella that she created was a cooler, more confident version of young Zoe Sugg. It doesn't matter how popular you are in real life or how many people you have annoyed or fallen out with; vlogging allows you to start again and create a new persona. Zoella isn't the only one to have done this. Jim Chapman appeared on camera in the BBC documentary *The Rise of the Superstar Vloggers*, saying: 'When I first started, I was twenty-two. I didn't have many friends. I was miserable. I'd say I started vlogging as an antisocial way of being sociable because you're just talking to a camera; you're not talking to real people. I felt I had more control. Straight away, I knew I loved it.'

Look carefully at some of the better-known vloggers and you'll see they have something else in common – super-high energy levels. In the majority of their videos, they are happy and enthusiastic. This energy is infectious, making viewers feel uplifted after watching the videos. Viewers are more likely to return if you've cheered up their day, watching more of your videos in the hope you'll do the same again. Remember that your viewers already have gloom and misery in their lives, and they're watching your videos for escapism. They don't want to waste time watching a video that projects negativity and, if you can't make upbeat and positive videos, viewers will start to look elsewhere and find other vloggers that can.

This doesn't mean you can only talk about positive subjects. Bad things happen to most people at some point, so you'll have to cover some tricky issues if you're being open and honest in your vlogs. But how you talk about the difficult subjects is important. If you act as if the world is against you, people won't warm to you. You have to come across as though you want things to get better, or hope they will.

Don't worry if you're not naturally enthusiastic and upbeat. It's hard to remain bright and sparkly for the duration of a YouTube video, but you can incorporate small things into your vlogging style to create a more energetic persona. Have you heard of the phrase 'telephone voice'? Some people talk differently when they're on the phone to when they're with someone face to face. This is because we use our facial expressions to help us communicate when we're in person, but not when we talk on the phone. As a result, our telephone voice has to be loud and clear. We enunciate our words more and speak more slowly, so the other person on the line can follow the conversation. In the same way, we need to think about our 'vlogging voice', because communicating with someone through a vlog is very different from communicating with someone face to face. When you're vlogging, you're talking to a viewer with a short attention span. Your viewers may be multi-tasking and watching a video while they do several other things. It's very different from having a conversation in real life, when the person you're talking to is alert and aware that they're expected to respond. There is no such pressure on a viewer. Once they've listened to you, they can walk away. They don't even have to wait until you're finished, and can switch off at any point. That's why you need to develop a vlogging voice that draws viewers into your video and captivates their attention so that leaving before the end is not an option.

One trick is to modulate your voice and place emphasis on key words. This will help you avoid sounding monosyllabic, which is the worst possible way to speak on camera if you want to attract an audience. Nobody wants to listen to someone drone on. It's boring and annoying!

You can practise modulation through repetition. Turn on your camera, place it in position and start talking. It doesn't matter whether what you're saying makes sense or not – just talk! When you're speaking, keep the pace high but enunciate every word. After you're comfortable with this, start placing emphasis on words that need emphasising while making sure to enunciate the rest of the words clearly.

You can also project energy through movement. Cast your mind back to watching TV as a child. Children's TV presenters are renowned for their energy and enthusiasm. Look closely, and you'll see they're always moving around. At times it seems like they're bouncing on the spot. They're also leaning in and leaning out of shot, and they pick up props or products with exaggerated movements. Look again at some of your favourite vloggers and you may see they use the same tactics!

You might also notice that your favourite vloggers always appear groomed and well-presented in their videos. Does this intimidate you? It shouldn't. You may think you're not as pretty or handsome as the vloggers you love to watch, but I'll let you into a little secret: it's easier to look good on camera than it is in real life. This is because you're in charge of the set and you can control the elements. You won't ruin your hair by getting rained on, and you don't have to hide behind frumpy, baggy jumpers in winter because you can adjust the heating on set.

When it comes to hair and fashion, you should take a bit of time to think about your target audience. How do they dress? Who are their style icons? What do these style icons wear? Your clothes should be similar, because you are aiming to make your viewers both relate to you and aspire to be like you.

I'm not suggesting you spend a fortune on the latest designer-clothing brands or get the most expensive haircut money can buy, but do look at what other people in your field are wearing and try to find similar items on the high street or online.

When it comes to hair, the current trend is long hair for both boys and girls, and you can style it yourself with no more than a hairdryer and some good hairspray. Alternatively, you could get a blow-dry once a week and film the videos when your hairdo is salon-fresh. The rest of the week you'll be editing and publicising the videos, and won't need to look as groomed.

If you're vlogging about a more serious subject, you may want to wear smart clothes or a suit. You wouldn't turn up for a job interview looking scruffy, would you? First impressions count. People will judge whether they like you or not before you've even opened your mouth – in interview situations and when they're watching your vlogs.

LOCATION, LOCATION, LOCATION

A lot of vloggers don't realise that creating a backdrop for their videos is almost as important as thinking about the theme that runs through them. This is because nobody will notice the theme if they can find fault with the setting. Viewers will notice if you've left dirty laundry lying around your room or if you haven't made the bed.

An ideal set is neat, stylish and contains cool elements in the background such as fairy lights, throws or artwork. However, don't overdo it on the background elements as too many props could distract viewers. You don't want people to spend too long looking at the background when you're talking in the foreground.

In essence, you're creating a mini TV set for yourself. Most vloggers choose to use the same set over and over again, as it creates brand repetition. If viewers see the same objects often enough, it starts to feel familiar and cosy, just like the Queen Vic on the TV soap *Eastenders* or the Rovers Return on *Coronation Street*. If viewers like your set, they're more likely to want to hang out in it and listen to what you have to say.

The location has to be somewhere you can control completely. Public spaces are generally a bad idea because you can't control passers-by or traffic noise. Also, some public spaces require a licence to film in. You may be able to come to an arrangement with a hotel or café, but bear in mind that they could change their minds at any time. Once you've built a following based on filming in a particular place, it's not ideal to have to find somewhere else because of circumstances beyond your control. For this reason, many vloggers start off by filming at home. There you can section off an area of the house and make it into a mini-studio. It doesn't matter how much mess or junk there is behind the camera as long as you can make up a tidy square in which to film yourself.

Think about what furniture you're going to have in the shot.

It's not a great idea to have a blank space, as viewers' attention will start to drift and they'll end up, quite literally, staring into space. What does your target market have in their houses? What would they like in their houses? You can also look at some of your favourite vloggers for inspiration. What are their sets like? Notice that none of them are near windows. While you may think this is ideal for lighting purposes, it brings up continuity issues as the sun is constantly changing position in the sky and could cause shadows. Windows are also very noisy due to weather sounds and the buzz of traffic outside. I'll discuss the important issues of light and sound in more detail in the next chapter.

When you've created a set, check to see how it looks on camera. Film the area on its own and with you sitting and performing in it. What looks great empty could appear cramped when you get started. Take a photo of it when you're happy. If you have a small room, you may want to pack the set away each time. The photo will ensure you remember where everything goes when you want to build it again. Viewers are very eagle-eyed when it comes to spotting inconsistencies.

Repetition increases brand awareness when it comes to location, name, logo and music. Once you've decided what you want to do, you have to keep doing it as you work through the rest of the chapters in this book.

After working through this chapter, you should have:

☐ Worked out a clever, catchy name for your vlog
☐ Designed a unique logo

Embrace Your Individuality

☐ Composed or picked a theme tune
☐ Thought about what you want to wear and how to do your hair
☐ Created a neat, stylish set that feels cosy and comfortable

CHAPTER 3

LIGHTS, CAMERA, ACTION!

Vlogging – unlike blogging – requires some start-up costs. You will need a camera, lighting, sound equipment and editing software, and these aren't cheap items. However, do you really think your favourite vloggers could afford state-of-the-art equipment when they started making videos? I can tell you for a fact that they didn't. Many of them were teenagers and bought basic equipment, which they learned to use well. They didn't upgrade to better gear until their videos started to bring in some money.

This chapter will explain how to minimise start-up costs and use what little equipment you have to make the best possible videos. No prior knowledge is necessary. It doesn't matter if you've never even switched on a camera before, let alone tried to frame a shot. Humans don't come out of the womb with a video camera in hand and an innate knowledge of what to do with it. Zoella, Alfie, KSI, Tanya and Jim have another thing in common – they all had to learn how to be filmmakers.

CAMERAS

Go to your favourite vlogger's YouTube channel and scroll back to look at the first videos they uploaded. Now look at a couple of recent ones. I bet you notice a huge difference in terms of camera quality, clarity of shot and perhaps even graininess.

In one of Zoella's first videos, eleven-year-old Zoe is presenting the contents of her suitcase before going on a family holiday. She's using a camcorder that is so out of date it could be in a museum. However, it still provides moving image and sound. She tries to improve the quality as much as possible by using the camera on a tripod to keep it steady and reduce blurriness. The video won't win any prizes for creative beauty, but it allows her to talk to an audience and start finding her vlogging voice.

The SBTV YouTube channel (youtube.com/smokeybarz) has almost 700,000 subscribers tuning in for beautifully shot music videos and interviews with artists. However, the quality of the videos wasn't always so high. The channel's founder Jamal Edwards started making videos on a cheap camera, which he received as a Christmas present when he was fifteen. He used that basic camera to film up-and-coming music acts in his area, quickly gaining a following from other music fans in his neighbourhood. He had no formal training and no fancy equipment, but he had a great deal of passion and was determined to teach himself as much as he could about filmmaking. As he started to earn money from his videos through YouTube advertising, he invested it in better camera gear and editing software, and hired other people to help him market the channel and spread the word. What started out as a basic operation with Jamal and a cheap camera turned into a business enterprise employing twelve staff by the time Jamal turned twenty-three – eight years after shooting his first video. SBTV now produces branded clothing and manages artists, and Jamal has started dipping his toes into charity work and politics. He can afford to as it's estimated he's now worth more than £8 million. The equipment he started with is irrelevant. What matters is that he used it to express his passion, knew who his audience were and filmed content that they enjoyed watching.

Have you heard the saying 'all gear and no idea'? It's used as an insult to describe someone who throws money at problems, thinking that buying the best equipment will make them a star. The reverse is true. The less time you spend shopping and the more time you spend learning how to use your kit, the more successful you will be. No matter what camera you have, you will improve your shot if you learn the following techniques.

FRAMING YOUR SHOT

In the previous chapter, we talked about using the same setting or location for all your videos. Your setting is called 'the background' in film speak, and you are 'the foreground'.

Make sure that the background is colourful, vibrant and exciting, as this adds atmosphere and makes people feel energised when they see the video. An empty set makes a video appear boring and lifeless, no matter how enthusiastic your voice sounds.

Also, make sure that you, in the foreground, are better lit than the background. Lighting controls where people look at the screen, and you want them to focus on what you're saying rather than looking at the set.

THE RULE OF THIRDS

Knowing the 'rule of thirds' will help make your videos more interesting and keep viewers engaged until the very end.

The rule of thirds states that the viewers' screen can be divided into three-by-three equal parts, totalling nine sections. The intersection point of any four of those sections forms an interest point for the human eye. Therefore, you need to frame objects of interest within these intersection points. Most importantly, make sure your eyes are framed within one of those intersections. Now work out where the other intersection points are, and make sure they're not empty. If you're not in one of these points, fill up the area with a poster, photos or fairy lights, as this will make your videos a lot more captivating.

The rule of thirds can be a hard concept to grasp when you're first starting out, as it takes time to be able to spot intersection points automatically. To keep things simple, find a white piece of paper or tracing paper and cut it to the same size as the screen of the computer you edit your videos on. Use a pen and ruler to draw nine equal boxes over the paper and affix it to your screen. Now go back to the set, get your background ready, jump into shot and film a small piece to camera. Play the footage back on the computer screen and look at where the objects in your set are in relation to the boxes on the grid. Are your eyes framed by an intersection? If not, you need to change where you sit on set. Are the other intersections full or empty? Change your set around until there is something in every point of intersection, i.e. every interest point.

CAMERA ANGLE, POSITION AND ZOOM

The positioning of your camera is vital. Camera angle refers to how high up the camera is in relation to the subject being filmed. Think about how you hold the camera when you take a selfie with your phone or digital camera. A good trick for a selfie is to hold the camera higher than you and angle it downwards so it's looking down on you. This angle will have a slimming effect, and it will also appear as if you have more defined cheekbones. Hold the camera below you and you're at risk of a double chin. This trick translates to video, meaning a more flattering shot will result if the camera is slightly above you. Alternatively, try the camera at eye level and see if you prefer that. You could use other angles at various points in your vlogs; for example, bird's eye view – where the camera is directly overhead – could be used to showcase products, or you could use a point-of-view (POV) angle – where you hold the camera so that it shows what you see – if you're reviewing an event. Once you've decided on your angles, you could experiment with different camera positions and degrees of zoom. For the most part, you'll probably be sat down facing the camera with your head and shoulders in shot, but you could try filming some footage with the camera off to one side, or zoomed in on your face or other items showcased in your vlogs. It's a good idea to mix it up and experiment – you could discover a really quirky or original use of the camera that will give your vlogs something extra. Remember to take into account the rule of thirds!

STABILITY

The best way to avoid a shaky shot is by using a tripod. If your videos feature a lot of movement, then you need a tripod with a lever that can be turned round smoothly. Jerky or sudden movements can kill the atmosphere of a video, as the viewer stops paying attention to what you're saying and starts to think about the camera. Once they've noticed an error, they start to pick holes in other aspects of the video. Unless viewers are fully happy with a video, they won't return to a channel to watch future vlogs. They'll find less jerky videos elsewhere and watch those instead of yours.

Fancy tripods are only needed by vloggers who make very animated videos. If your videos largely consist of you talking to the camera, you just need a base that will hold the camera so it doesn't fall over and get damaged. Many vloggers use Gorillapods, which are flexible and bendy tripods that cost between £10 and £20 from online stores like Amazon. You can mould them into whatever shape you want and put them on a shelf or a desk. They're very small and won't take up much room in your house, which is useful if you don't have much space for your set and equipment.

Once you've mastered these basic techniques, the amount of further knowledge you need depends on what camera you have. For example, if you have a DSLR you will need to put a lot of time into figuring out what all the features do and what lenses you should use. A lot of vloggers prefer to start with an entry-level camera and graduate to a DSLR later on, because they'd rather focus on creating awesome content than work out what different aperture and white-balance settings mean.

I advise starting with a good-value point-and-shoot camera, so you can practise framing shots using the rule of thirds and angling the camera to show your most flattering side. You'll save money if you do some research before you buy! The YouTube channel DailyTekk (youtube.com/DailyTekk) specialises in reviewing camera gear, and a recent video suggested that the most popular entry-level cameras are:

Canon Powershot G7 X: Vloggers love this camera because of the screen on the back, which flips up so you can see yourself as you're shooting. It's also a touchscreen so you can easily zoom in for close-ups. It's brilliant in low lighting, and the image stabilisation is impressive for such an inexpensive camera. Professional vlogger Casey Neistat (youtube.com/caseyneistat) takes a Canon G7 X everywhere he goes, and makes videos mixing 'on-location' shots that he's taken on the G7 X with static shots that he's filmed on a DSLR. He has 2.6 million subscribers. The ultimate technology vlogger iJustine (youtube.com/ijustine) also uses a Canon Powershot G7 X and recently dedicated a whole vlog to its features. Type 'iJustine' and 'Canon G7 X' into Google and her video will be first in the search results. It's worth watching if you're thinking about getting a new camera.

Sony Cyber-shot RX100: This camera is similar to the Canon G7 X as it also has a pop-up screen. It has the same sensor as the Canon Powershot G7 X, making it capable in low light, and its compact size makes it easy to carry around. The Sony camera tends to be quieter than the G7 X when shooting and has a longer battery life. It comes with built-in Wi-Fi so you can upload your videos to your computer without any cables, and reviewers suggest it's the closest thing you'll get to a DSLR without actually buying one. These extra features come with a catch – the Sony RX100 is more expensive than the Canon G7 X.

GoPro HERO4 Black: This camera is favoured by vloggers covering sports events and those trying to be more creative with their set-up. It has wide-angle and time-lapse modes, which you can use to create a unique style of video, and it shoots in 4K resolution so your videos will still be relevant in a few years' time when 1080p resolution is a thing of the past. Its microphone is ideal for vloggers who are moving around or on the go. However, the most useful feature is its durability: you can take this camera over rugged terrain without damaging it. If you want to see why the GoPro HERO4 Black is so popular with action-sports vloggers, check out Ty Moss's YouTube channel (youtube.com/tymoss).

Samsung NX Mini: The Samsung NX Mini has all the features of the Canon and Sony models such as a 180-degree flip-screen, the ability to film in 1080p HD resolution, an amazing CMOS sensor and built-in Wi-Fi. However, the advantage it has over the other makes is that it's a third of the cost. It's also a third of the size at just 22.5mm thick, so it looks pretty stylish when you pull it out of your pocket.

iPhone 6: An iPhone 6 can shoot 60 frames a second, making it better quality than some digital cameras. However, it's more suited to static shots as it doesn't have the same image stabilisation as the Canon, Samsung and Sony models, and you're likely to see a lot of shaking if you try to film moving footage. It works best when used with a tripod or a stand to hold it still as you talk to the camera in your house or bedroom. You can buy external lenses and lighting for it pretty cheaply, as well as an external microphone to improve sound quality. It's not ideal, but it means you don't have to worry if you really can't afford a new camera.

LIGHTING

If you've ever had the chance to visit a television or movie set, you'll have noticed the amount of lighting equipment they have. A set designer has taken the time to create the perfect set, and the correct lighting ensures TV audiences can see every single detail of the set and the people on it. You don't need to invest in the same kit used by the professionals, but you do need to ensure you have a couple of extra lights in your room so that your face and body are well lit. Darkness is unflattering. You've spent time thinking about what clothes you're going to wear and how you're going to do your hair, so you must use lighting to ensure that viewers can see you in all your glory. Darkness also means dullness, and a dark set can destroy the atmosphere of a video or hurt a viewer's eyes as they squint at the screen trying to make out what's going on. Both of these will put the viewer off from subscribing to your channel.

The type of lighting you need depends on how close you will be to the screen. Beauty vloggers tend to do a lot of close-ups, so they need to use just one light source. This tends to be a ring light. A ring light is a hollow circle of light, within which your camera sits. Ring lights project light exactly where you need them: since beauty vloggers tend to be looking at the camera when they're talking, the light around the camera illuminates their face perfectly. You can always tell when a vlogger has used a ring light as there is a ring reflection in the irises of their eyes. Have a look at your favourite beauty vloggers and see if you can spot it. Established vloggers Vivianna Does Makeup (youtube. com/ viviannadoesmakeup) and Lily Pebbles (youtube.com/ WhatIHeartToday) have both made videos where they talk about using a ring light. Lily Pebbles says: 'One of the main things I like about the ring light is how small and easy to move around it is. As well as being small, the light it gives is very flattering and you get that diva light circle in your eyes (if you want it). I now use this all the time instead of a softbox or another lamp.'

Ring lights can vary in price, but you don't need top-of-the-range gear at the start of your vlogging career. All you need is a ring light that specifies it's set to 5500K or 6500K. This means the ring mimics natural light as opposed to giving off a yellowish or beige tinge like a lightbulb or a lamp. Bright white lights are much more flattering than darker yellow bulbs. Look on Amazon or eBay for a good deal and you should be able to get a decent-quality one for less than £100.

If you are going to be some distance away from the camera or moving around, then you'll need more lighting to illuminate different parts of your set. These lights should be set up in a way known to the filmmaking trade as 'three -point lighting'. This sounds very technical, but is a fancy way of reminding you to place your lights in a triangular shape around the set. You want a light off to each side and one in front of you. However, the triangle should be angled so the tip is not directly in front of you. Your three lights need to be placed as follows.

First light: In front of you to light your face but slightly to the right side.

Second light: Directly to the left side of you but slightly in front.

Third light: Directly to the right side of you but slightly behind you.

The light in front of you will reflect in your eyes and the light behind you will give depth to the video. The other side light should help to fill in and eliminate shadows.

It's vital to use the same type of light for each of the three points, e.g. three desk lamps or three specialised photography lights. This is because different gear emits different coloured lights – some are warm, some cool and some fluorescent. You will get some odd effects if you mix warm lighting with cool lighting.

In addition, you might want to consider using a softbox, which is a device used to diffuse light by bouncing it from a light surface (usually white or silver fabric). The diffuse light given from a softbox is very flattering and helps to eliminate shadows.

It doesn't matter what you use – lamps, softboxes or LED lights – as long as the three lights are the same. Use what's available in your house or what you can borrow from another vlogger to keep costs down at the start. You can upgrade once money is coming in from advertising and other sources.

If you want to check that you're applying three-point lighting in the best possible way, you could do a little experiment. Start by filming a short video with no additional lighting. Then film with one of your lights on, two of your lights on and then switch on all three. You should notice the quality of the video is best when all three lights are on and that it's a big improvement on no lighting at all, even if you're just using three adjustable desk lamps.

SOUND

Now you've worked out how to look the best you can on screen through a clear shot and adequate lighting, make sure that viewers can hear what you're saying.

The quality of the in-built microphone on modern cameras is constantly improving, so you won't need to purchase an external microphone unless you plan on shooting outside. If you're simply talking to a camera while sat inside your house, then the microphones on a Canon G7 X or Sony Cyber-shot RX100 are more than capable.

For outside shots, a camera's built-in microphone isn't the best as it always picks up the closest sound. This could be wind or traffic noises if you're filming outside, making the background sounds appear louder than your voice. The only way to solve the problem is to move the camera closer to your face, defeating the point of being outside as viewers will only see your face and not the scenery. This is why vloggers who do lots of pranking, comedy or action-sports videos while out and about tend to ignore the audio function on their camera and use a portable digital recorder to capture sound. These look like dictaphones, they're usually very small and they can be hidden in clothing to ensure they're being held as close as possible to your mouth while remaining out of shot of the camera. You can also ask a good friend to assist you for the day and hold the portable mic close to you but out of shot.

The popular vlogging website Vlogger Pro (vloggerpro.com) recommends the Zoom H1 portable audio device to vloggers starting out because of its low price point and impressive technical capabilities. It will help you create great-quality recordings thanks to its two overlapping unidirectional microphones. This feature means that you will get an accurate stereo recording of your voice while minimising background noise. You can also buy a furry hat for the recorder which will help reduce the buffeting sounds created by wind. The Zoom H1 Handy Recorder is currently priced at £89 on Amazon (amazon.co.uk) but it will make your videos feel a million times more professional.

If it's a very windy day or you're worried about where to put the audio device, consider investing in a lapel mic (also known as a 'lavalier mic'). You clip these tiny microphones to your clothing and attach a belt-pack transmitter to your body, usually in a back pocket. Then you plug a wireless receiver into the mic input on your portable recorder to pick up the transmissions coming from the belt-pack. You need to make sure that the transmitter and receiver have fresh batteries, both are powered on, and that the lavalier mic isn't rubbing against your clothing or picking up any wind noise. They're very small, so it's easy to clip them to clothing, and you can put the wireless transmitter with your audio device anywhere that's out of shot, such as your handbag or camera bag.

As lavalier mics are available for prices as low as £40 on Amazon, you can achieve professional-quality sound very cheaply. Audio-Technica lavalier mics are currently very popular as the belt-pack transmitter is tiny, making it easy to stash on your person without it being in shot.

Once you've finished recording audio on a portable device or with the lavalier set-up, you'll need to sync it up with the visuals when you come to the video edit. This is known as 'double-system' shooting. It's important to match it up correctly because viewers will be put off if they see your lips moving ahead of or behind the words that you appear to be saying. There's one trick you can apply to make syncing easier – clap your hands. Do this before you start speaking, then match the sound of the clap with the visual in your edit. If you get the clap right, the sound of your voice will sync with the movement of your lips perfectly.

TIP: GET SOME WORK EXPERIENCE

Do you know any vloggers or filmmakers who are more experienced than you? Ask if you can shadow them for a day, or help them out by running errands for them while they're filming. It will give you a chance to see what kit they use and how they use it.

In this chapter, the kit recommended is:

☐ Canon Powershot G7 X: available at John Lewis, Amazon or Canon for £350–£400
☐ Sony Cyber-shot RX 100: available at Jessops, Amazon or Sony for £250–£300

- [ ] GoPro HERO4 Black: available at John Lewis, Jessops or GoPro online for £320–£400
- [ ] Samsung NX Mini: available at Tesco, Amazon or John Lewis for £170–£200
- [ ] Neewer ring light: available at Amazon from £77
- [ ] Zoom H1 Handy Recorder: available at Amazon for £89
- [ ] Audio-Technica lapel microphones: available at Amazon from £25

CHAPTER 4

KISS – KEEP IT SHORT AND SWEET!

What is the best length for a vlog? There is no one-size-fits-all answer to this question and it largely depends on the type of content you are creating. News and politics vlogs tend to be longer than beauty and lifestyle vlogs, as more in-depth analysis is required in order to present the content in an educational way. It also depends on the audience that you are aiming at. Younger people may have shorter attention spans than those who are over fifty, and they could have distractions such as homework, social media, part-time jobs and other TV and YouTube viewing habits.

In previous chapters, we've looked at vlogging experts such as Zoella, Alfie Deyes, Tanya Burr, Jim Chapman, ThatcherJoe and Caspar Lee, and picked out things they have in common. We can do the same to work out how long our videos should be. Go to your favourite vlogger's channel and pick out five videos at random. You should notice that they're not all the same length. Sometimes they're as short as two minutes and at other times they can go on for as long as five minutes. One of the benefits of vlogging is you can stop when you run out of things to say. You're not on TV, filling a timed link between segments, so there is no pressure to talk for a specific length of time. It's good to keep viewers on their toes as there's more chance they will get bored if your vlogs always follow the same rigid format.

Were you bored at any time while watching one of your favourite vloggers' videos? The answer should be no, as this is what separates professional vloggers from amateur vloggers – they know when to shut up. If they don't have anything to say, then they'll make a short video, and if they know they can keep someone's attention for a longer period, they'll let the video run on. During the editing process, they'll review the video objectively and cut out any waffle. Whether their vlogs last two minutes or five minutes, everything they talk about during that time is relevant to the video's storyline.

Very few videos made by your favourite vlogger will be longer than five minutes in duration. This is because it's hard to keep people's attention when they're watching YouTube, and the longer a video lasts, the more likely it is that viewers will get distracted and switch off. Video analytics service Wistia has closely monitored some top YouTube channels and found that, on average, videos lasting four to five minutes result in fewer than 60 per cent of viewers watching the entire video, against 75 per cent for a one- to two-minute video. The most successful vloggers are aware that, if they want their viewers to stick with them until the final call to action, they need to keep their videos short and sweet.

Enter 'popular on YouTube' into Google, and the first result will be a YouTube channel featuring the week's most popular videos – from movie trailers to cute animal videos. I've monitored this channel carefully over three months, and I've noticed that most of its videos tend to be two to three minutes or three to four minutes in length. There are very few longer than four minutes, and even fewer longer than five. Keeping videos short and sweet works for anyone making content for YouTube, not just vloggers.

So how do you keep videos short and to the point? If you've ever switched a camera on and talked down the lens, you'll know how easy it is to go off-subject. As you talk about one topic, it might lead you to think of a similar experience, and you might mention it even though it's not strictly relevant to the storyline of that vlog. It's easy enough to cut this out during the editing process, but wouldn't it be easier if you didn't get distracted in the first place?

I'll let you into a little secret: most vloggers script their videos. This helps them to stay on track during filming, meaning less work during the editing process. You may argue that you want to vlog about your daily life and capture people's reactions to things as they happen, and that having a script will make your footage appear artificial and rigid. This doesn't have to be the case, as there are different levels of scripting. Some vloggers might write a full script, whereas others will just have a vague plan written in bullet points. But they've all thought about what elements their videos will contain.

This is largely because interesting and funny things don't happen that often in life. You may have a fun-packed Friday where you grab lunch with a friend, go shopping, indulge in some beauty treatments and hang out with your mates at a party, but what happens if Monday is no more action-packed than going to school or work, then eating dinner? People will only want to watch your videos if they are more exciting than their own lives. It's a good idea to take time out at the start of the week to plan some activities, then you can space out these activities and be confident that you'll be able to produce an entertaining video each day. John Carle, Director of Network Development for Collective Digital Studio, which manages US vloggers, explains: 'The most recent stat I heard was that there are three hundred hours of content being uploaded every minute to YouTube. But at the same time, the amount of content watched by the majority of the audience is microscopic in comparison. So it really does come down to whether you are making something that is connecting with your audience. If you're connecting with that audience, they'll keep coming back to you regardless of the other two hundred and ninety-nine hours.' The way to connect with your audience is to keep them entertained and captivated by the fun you're having in your videos.

While you're planning what to do each week, think about some funny anecdotes or facts related to each topic. What are you trying to communicate to the viewer by letting them into that aspect of your life? What does the activity mean to you and why? You'll be tempted to say 'umm' and 'errr' if you start filming without an idea of why you're shooting, and this makes you look stupid. If you ramble on about a subject without saying anything useful or interesting about it, then you'll look shallow. People aren't interested in watching you if you're not better than them in at least some way, and they'll switch off if they feel they are more articulate than you.

Having a script does not lead to extra pressure to learn lines. When you're vlogging, you can pause the camera as much as you want to look over your script. It doesn't matter even if you mess up a line, as there are no costs involved in retakes. It's not like TV, where retakes require rehiring actors, hair, make-up and camera crew. You can film shots as many times as you want on however many days you want until you get the shot with the right amount of energy and enthusiasm. Some people will argue that the first take is the most 'natural', but what if you wanted to improve on the natural you? Sometimes you'll have more enthusiasm in your voice and a more energetic tone in the second or third take. Keep going until you know you have something you're proud of.

Have you ever written a script before? I find the process becomes easier if you divide it into three steps. If you want to keep your planning loose and more improvised, you can stop after the first step. Many experienced vloggers stop after step two as they have a lot of relevant things to say about their subject matter after years of making videos on the same topic. However, try all three steps if you're new to vlogging as it will make you feel more prepared and give you confidence in front of the camera.

STEP ONE: RESEARCH!

What do you want to communicate by making this video? What do you need to show to communicate your points? Think about each thing you'll be showing and research it extensively, using multiple reference points. For example, you might be a beauty vlogger wanting to communicate how to achieve a smoky eye make-up look. To get your point across, you'll need to show eyeshadow, mascara and eyeliner techniques. Find out different types of products you can use and what ingredients they contain. Investigate whether some products are easier to apply than others and look at how much they cost. You can use all of these facts in your videos. You might be a fashion vlogger wanting to communicate the most on-trend looks this season. You'll need to show some different outfits. What stores can you get them from? Is there a budget version and a luxury version? Are any celebrities wearing similar outfits?

If you're planning to stop here, you don't need to write anything down as long as you're confident you have soaked up enough knowledge to be able to inform your viewers. However, it may help to make notes so you can re-read them before you start filming. This will give you the confidence to know that you have plenty of information available if you freeze in front of the camera. If you're continuing to step two and step three, then you should definitely write things down.

STEP TWO: ORGANISE YOUR NOTES!

Start with a fresh piece of paper and list the topics you'll be covering in your video, leaving a large gap in between each entry. To go back to the beauty example, this would be eyeliner, eyeshadow and mascara.

Now re-read your original research notes and underline the

most important facts and figures. List these in order of priority underneath the relevant topic. For example, under the mascara heading you might write notes about application tactics, price and stockists.

Will you talk about the topics in the order you've listed on the sheet? If not, write a number next to each topic to remind you of the sequence. For beauty videos, this will be determined by the order in which you apply the make-up. For gaming videos, if you want to list your top five tips, the order should start with the most useful tip, followed by the next most useful and so on.

Think about your intro and outro. Jot down some prompts for your intro that sum up what your video is about. For the outro, write down some calls to action so you don't forget to ask people to subscribe and comment.

Finally, you should consider where you will position the camera for each topic. Note that down next to the relevant topic, using a different-coloured pen so it stands out from your facts and figures. Use the same-coloured pen to note down any props you're going to use. Viewers will get bored of you talking to the camera after a short time, even if you've practised sounding energetic and enthusiastic, so you need to mix up your footage. One way to mix it up is by using props such as make-up products, and filming close-ups of the products as you explain what they are. You could also use pie-charts or graphics to demonstrate a specific trend. Or you could add variety by demonstrating what you're talking about and mixing shots of talking to camera with the demos in your edit.

Many vloggers choose to stop here, to make their videos a mix of drafted scripting and some natural presentation. As you're not writing down full sentences next to the topics, you have some flexibility with what you say, which makes it sound like you're naturally knowledgeable.

STEP THREE: FLESH OUT THE DRAFT!

If you complete this step, you can be sure that your videos are densely populated with useful information. This is a huge confidence boost for anyone starting out, because nerves have a terrible habit of making your mind go blank. With a full script on the side, just out of shot, you have something to refer to in between takes.

The most recent list you made should contain all the facts and figures along with relevant camera angles and positions, so all you have to do is flesh it out and add some sentences to link everything. Think about how you would say something and write it down exactly as you'd speak it, so you sound natural and not as if you're reciting an essay. Try and think of jokes or interesting ways of saying things, so that you can show viewers you are fun, witty and entertaining.

Once you have a full script, you can run through it a few times before turning on the camera. This will help you work out where pauses need to be for dramatic effect, and which words you need to emphasise. Use a pencil to underline these words, then you can refer to your script during filming to remind yourself of your lines and the modulation needed. If you plan on using several camera angles and positions, there will be plenty of time to re-read your script after each time you move the camera.

TIP: MAKE SURE YOUR VIDEOS CONTAIN
A PROBLEM AND A SOLUTION

An easy way to divide your points into a beginning, middle and end while adding some drama and keeping your viewers' attention is to follow this structure:

Intro: Identify yourself and hook viewers in with a sentence that sums up the topic of the vlog. Then promise something that will keep them watching, such as a tip you'll reveal later or a special offer that you'll give them at the end.

Problem: Identify a problem that your viewers may have. Be honest and open about your own problems and experiences with this topic. By introducing a problem, you can offer a solution. Viewers will feel more involved with your video if you're solving one of their issues.

Solution: This is the key part of the video. Your solution needs to be simple and concise. Break down the concepts and explain everything in a way that will make sense to anyone watching. Great vloggers have an ability to cover complex subjects and break them down in a way that is fun, entertaining and easy for anyone to understand or copy. This applies especially to the best beauty vloggers, who manage to make complicated make-up tricks simpler, thus giving people at home more confidence.

Summary: What is the main thing you want people to take home from this video? Summarise this into one sentence. You can also have this as a graphic on screen, written as a list or summed up in a subtitle at the bottom of the screen.

Call to action: Make your viewers feel important by asking them to connect with you further. Invite viewers to leave a specific comment below your video (and ensure you enable comments on your blog post if you plan to embed the vlog into a blog post). Sometimes, vloggers sound like they're begging when they ask for subscribers, and this is off-putting because nobody wants to subscribe to someone who's desperate. The way to encourage subscriptions is to suggest there's something in it for the viewers. You could say something like: 'For more exclusive tips and to stay up to date with the latest news, you need to subscribe.'

Writing a script will also help you stay on track when you have to cover personal subjects. The best vloggers are very honest and share details of their lives and feelings with their viewers. This helps the viewers get to know the vloggers better, so the viewers start to see the vlogger as a friend. However, the more emotional a vlogger is about a subject, the more chance they have of breaking down and forgetting what to say, or going off on a tangent and ranting about a topic that's not directly relevant. You can prepare yourself for these tricky videos by writing down why you want to make the vlog and listing some points that further explain your motivation. Then you'll feel more confident when you start talking as you know your notes are waiting at the side if you get stuck.

CASE STUDY: GRACIE FRANCESCA

Gracie has 205,000 subscribers to her YouTube channel Grace F Victory (youtube.com/UglyFaceOfBeauty). In her videos, she talks frankly about her battles with mental health and eating disorders, and a vlog about her treatment in a psychiatric ward received more than 250,000 views.

She says: 'It's important to showcase the other side of you. Viewers like to see how your life is. So, if you feel like you want to cry, then cry. If you're having a bad day, then show that you're having a bad day.

'They say that the two most important days in your life are when you're born and when you realise why. One day, I had an email from a lady whose daughter was in hospital on her deathbed. She had anorexia. That lady wrote to me and said I'd saved her daughter's life, and that her daughter was watching my videos and getting better and slowly gaining weight. That's the day I realised why I'm here, and it is to help people and change people's views.'

CASE STUDY: BECKY SHEERAN, TALKBECKYTALK

Becky quit her job as a trainee BBC TV presenter to focus on YouTube full-time. Her YouTube channel TalkBeckyTalk (youtube.com/TalkBeckyTalk) has more than 160,000 sub-scribers. She debated whether or not to cover in her vlogs the subject of her father's sudden death, but found being honest with her audience helped her cope.

She says: 'I sat in front of the camera and talked. The support I got was incredible. My viewers got me through the hardest months of my life. We had thousands and thousands of letters and emails of support every single day. It got to the point where I walked along the street and someone would say, "I watched one of your videos and I want to give you a hug because of your dad." It was so emotional to go through that with them.'

Don't throw away your script once you've finished filming. It will speed up the editing process if you have the script to hand when you're working out which scenes to cut, because you'll have written down the most important things. If something's not on your script, cut it out to Keep It Short and Simple. K.I.S.S.

By the end of this chapter, you should have:

☐ Researched the length of your favourite vloggers' videos
☐ Researched the subjects you're covering in your vlog
☐ Soaked up knowledge related to those subjects
☐ Planned a beginning, middle and end to hook in viewers and solve their problems
☐ Thought about camera angles and props to illustrate key points

CHAPTER 5

EDIT LIKE A PRO

Having the right editing software and knowing how to use it is just as important as picking appropriate filming equipment and shooting enough takes until you like how you come across. Getting good footage is useless if you don't know how to edit it to make a professional-looking vlog.

In Chapter 3 I brought up the concept of 'all gear and no idea', and suggested it was more important to learn how to use your camera and lighting kit than to shop for state-of-the-art equipment. The same applies when it comes to editing software. It doesn't matter how much you spend buying industry-standard packages, such as Final Cut Pro X or Adobe Premiere Pro, if you're not aware of some basic editing techniques. In this chapter, I will talk you through some specific features of Final Cut Pro and Adobe Premiere Pro, as well as Apple's iMovie and

Windows Movie Maker, but first you need to know these key editing tips.

REFER TO YOUR SCRIPT

When you're filming, your brain is occupied with getting each take right and it's easy to lose track of your overall vision. Before you start editing your video, it's a good idea to refer to your original notes or full script to remind yourself of how you wanted the finished video to look. This will make you more decisive when it comes to working out what scenes to cut and where you may need additions like subtitles or graphics to emphasise your points.

AVOID FANCY TRANSITIONS

A simple way to spot the difference between an amateur vlogger and a seasoned pro is to look at the special effects they have or haven't used in the edit. Amateurs often think they have to spin the screen around or fade in and out between scenes, whereas successful vloggers appreciate the power of keeping things simple. Complex transitions grab viewers' attention and take it away from the content of the video. The only cut you need when editing a vlog is the 'jump cut'.

Jump cuts get their name from how they cause the person on screen to appear to jump from one position to another. Usually, this is a subtle movement, but viewers can tell that the speaker's mouth and face has slightly moved position. The amateur nature of a jump cut is part of its appeal. Smooth transitions are expected in film and television because of the amount of resources available, but vlogging has a more homemade quality to it. Viewers prefer vlogs that look homemade and authentic because they feel more realistic.

Jump cuts also increase the perceived speed with which someone conveys information, emotion and fun, so that the content comes at you faster and feels more stimulating. It takes time to spin a screen round or use a fade effect, and that slows down the pace of a video. There are no limits to how many jump cuts you can use in a video because they're so quick. They're a great tool for removing the 'umms' and 'errrs' you may have said if you weren't too clear on your script. This will keep your videos energetic and waffle-free.

Let's work through an example of how a jump cut might be used in a video. Imagine you've turned the camera on, sat down and got comfy, and started by saying: 'To create the perfect red lipstick, I always start by lining my lips with this pencil. Errr, my pencil needs sharpening. Let me sharpen it. So, I like this liner because it's a gorgeous cherry red.' You've become distracted and gone off track. Your video will sound pacier if you cut it after the first time you say 'pencil' until 'I like this liner because…'

The following steps show how to create a jump cut in iMovie, but other programmes will be similar.

Step one: Import your video into your editing software and drag it to the timeline. Make sure you can see the audio file as well as the visual file. If everything appears together, find the tool entitled *Detach Audio*. The audio should appear on your editing screen in a wave file.

Step two: Play the clip to decide which parts you want to cut out and which you want to keep. The first part you should cut is the part where you're sitting down and trying to get comfortable. How many beauty bloggers have you watched who begin their videos by sitting down? None! They get straight to it.

The start of your video should be the part where you say, 'To create the perfect red lipstick…' To cut it, look at the audio file rather than the visual file as this will show you when the sound starts. You don't want to cut out too much and start halfway through the sentence, but it would be very easy to do so if you looked only at the visual file.

Place your cursor as close to the beginning of the sound on the wave file as possible. Click *Split Clip*. Now delete the part before the split by selecting it and right-clicking for delete, or by using one of the options in the menu bar.

Step three: Where is the next cut? It should be just after 'pencil'. Again, you need to watch the wave file. Place your cursor as close to the end of the sound of 'pencil' as possible and split.

Step four: Play on until you find the next bit you want to keep. This will be before the word 'I' and after the word 'so'. Place your cursor as close as you can to the start of the sound of 'I' and split.

Step five: The bit in the middle is the bit with all the useless information in it. Delete it!

Now, when you play the two clips together, you have an excellent, pacy jump-cut edit. Repeat these steps for the rest of the footage until you've removed all the rubbish bits and you have a slick vlog.

The key thing to remember is to pay attention to the audio wave file rather than the visual file.

TIP: LOOK FOR VIDEOS EXPLAINING JUMP CUTS

There are some awesome video tutorials explaining jump cuts on YouTube. These demonstrate how to cut the audio file as close as possible to the words you want and enable you to watch someone else going through the whole process. You could do the practical bits at the same time as the demonstrator, pausing the video while you follow the steps outlined.

Check out ReelSEO's YouTube channel (YouTube.com/ reelzeo). Find the jumpcut video on this channel by typing 'jump cut' into the channel search box. This is located above the featured video and is one of the subheadings next to *Videos, Playlists, Channels, Discussion* and *About.*

MAKE A SET INTRO

It will save time if you create a set intro and save it to your desktop, ready to insert into all your videos. It can be as simple as a three-second clip of your logo accompanied by some free music, or it can be as complicated as a custom-made animation. The only thing that matters is that it grabs people's attention in less than five seconds. Also, you want it to sound upbeat so that your video begins on an energetic note.

TIP: USE AN ONLINE INTRO-BUILDING SERVICE

There are several great online services that you can use to create an introduction with your vlog's logo.

Intro Maker (intromaker.net): This offers a few different

---

video options. Some are free, but most range from $5 to $20. After uploading your logo, you pay via PayPal and the finished video is emailed to your PayPal email address.

Splasheo (splasheo.com/products): There are twenty logo animations available here to make your logo come to life. Once you've decided on an animation, you need to choose one of six audio options: *rock, happy, inspirational, cinematic, hip-hop* or *no music at all.* Videos cost $47, and, once you've paid, you will be able to customise the animation by uploading your logo.

ADD SOME MUSIC

Music helps to create a mood, enhance energy and cover up background noise. However, it's very important to get royalty-free music, or your video could get removed from YouTube and your account suspended altogether.

In December 2014, YouTube announced that its Audio Library had a new feature enabling vloggers to see exactly what would happen if they used copyrighted material in their videos. This means you can see whether your video will be taken down or whether ads will be disabled.

In general, it's not a good idea to use copyrighted music, as all the ad revenue from the video you've worked so hard to make will go to the copyright holders of the music. If you want to 'get rich vlogging', you don't want to hand over money to anyone else!

Fortunately, there are several online libraries that you can visit to find low-cost or free music. They include:

- **Incompetech** (incompetech.com)
- **DanoSongs** (danosongs.com)
- **Partners In Rhyme** (partnersinrhyme.com)
- **Free Soundtrack Music** (freesoundtrackmusic.com)
- **ccMixter** (ccmixter.org)
- **Musopen** (musopen.org)
- **RoyaltyFreeMusic** (royaltyfreemusic.com)

Incompetech is the site most vloggers go to first, as composer Kevin MacLeod has created a vast selection of soundtracks from horror to polka to rock and everything in between. The site also makes it really simple to find the right atmosphere for a video project, as tracks are categorised by genre and feel. If you want your sound to be energetic, you can search for energetic music. If you want something more sombre, you can search for that too.

When using music in a video, ensure that the volume of the music is lower than the volume of your voice. Avoid using music with lyrics when you're speaking, as that will confuse the viewer and give them a headache as their brain struggles to focus. Opt for beat-based or classical music instead.

INSERT IMAGES AND INFOGRAPHICS

Remember that the best vlogs are always concise (Keep It Short and Sweet) and that images can be worth a thousand words. The right image can explain what you want to communicate quicker than you can say it, so it's worthwhile thinking about whether inserting images and infographics in the editing process could help you cut your video down.

If so, it's best to create your own images and infographics to avoid copyright restrictions. YouTube does have a Fair Use policy, under which there are four terms in which video creators can get away with using copyrighted material without the owners' permission, but it is long-winded and open to various interpretations. See for yourself by reading the policy, which can be found by scrolling down to the bottom of the YouTube homepage and clicking on *Copyright*, which is next to *About* and *Press*. To avoid doubt, take your own photos, use royalty-free images and create your own infographics.

Have you ever used an infographic before? An infographic is visual representation of data, usually in the form of pie-charts, graphs or flowcharts. Not all vloggers need infographics, and they are rarely used in fashion or beauty vlogs, for example, but you may need them if you're planning a politics- or current affairs-based vlog. The following websites will help you:

- **Piktochart** (piktochart.com)
- **Venngage** (venngage.com)
- **Infogr.am** (infogr.am)

Most vloggers would benefit from royalty-free photos to illustrate a topic. Royalty-free photos can be found on these websites:

- **123RF** (123rf.com)
- **iStock** (istockphoto.com)
- **Pixabay** (pixabay.com)

- **Everystockphoto** (everystockphoto.com)
- **Creative Commons** (search.creativecommons.org)

When using these sites, read the terms and conditions under each image carefully. Sometimes you are required to credit the photographer, which you must do in the video or the video description box on YouTube.

SAVE FREQUENTLY

Whatever software you decide to use, don't forget to save at regular intervals. Video editing software can be temperamental, and you don't want to lose your hard work if it crashes.

APPLE IMOVIE

There's a joke which runs 'once you go Mac, you never go back', but for many vloggers it's more than a joke – it's a motto for life. Sales of Apple laptops and desktops increase each quarter, while PC sales have been declining for years. According to *TechRadar* magazine, 23 million Mac laptop or desktop units were sold in 2015, more than a 10 per cent increase from the 19.9 million units sold the year before. In contrast, sales of PCs declined by 3 per cent. For this reason, let's start with Apple's free editing software iMovie, and then cover the free PC editing software made by Windows in the next section.

Many vloggers start out using iMovie as it has all the features needed to put together a decent quality vlog, and it's free software installed on every Mac laptop and desktop.

These are the iMovie functions you need to know about:

IMPORT MOVIE

When you open up the iMovie programme, you'll see a Project Library at the top left of the screen, an Event Library at the bottom left and a preview screen at the top right. The option to import the video is in the Event Library, signposted by a heading at the top of the Event Library screen.

To import iMovie projects or other videos that are stored on your hard drive, select a file – or Command and click to select multiple files – and drag them from your desktop to an Event in the list on the left-hand side of the Event Library screen. By the way, these files need not be just video files; you can grab photos and audio files too and drag them to the same Event.

Alternatively, you could use the menu bar at the very top of the iMovie screen to import video. Choose *File >Import Media*, and it will automatically create a new Event in the Event Library.

START A NEW PROJECT

Every time you edit a video, you'll be starting with a blank canvas. This is what's known as a New Project.

Use the main menu at the top of the iMovie screen to choose *File >New Project*. When you click on *New Project*, a drop-down menu will appear at the top with many different themes and options. For your first project I would highly recommend selecting *No Theme*. You want to focus on getting the content right before adding anything fancy that could detract from what's inside the video.

To the right, you have a few important settings. First, you will need to name your project. Use one word that sums up what the video is about and an abbreviation of the date it was filmed.

Second, you have an option to select the aspect ratio, either widescreen (16:9) or standard (4:3). Here you must select the format in which your videos were filmed. This can be confirmed in your camera's settings, but most new cameras film in widescreen. YouTube is optimised for widescreen footage so, if you have the choice, always film in widescreen.

Third, you have the frame rate and a choice between NTSC, PAL or Cinema. This setting is usually determined by your geographical location and may be set by default. Most cameras from North America are NTSC, and in Europe most cameras are the PAL format. The final format, Cinema, is a type of video format which has become popular again in recent years and comes as an option with newer cameras. It's also more difficult to work with, so my advice is to stick to NTSC or PAL.

The final option is whether or not you want to automatically add transitions. I wouldn't recommend this, as you can always add different transitions later on if you decide your video needs it. Most don't.

After creating your project, a timeline will appear in the top-left corner enabling you to start adding edited video to your movie. This is where you will drag clips from your imported work, after you have removed the 'errrs' and 'umms' with jump cuts.

EDITING IMPORTED VIDEO
Click on the video name in the Event Library and it will show up in a large window at the bottom right of the screen. Now you

have to cut out all the waffle and make the good bits shine by adding music and images. It's not easy, but you can break it down into nine steps. Do your best at each stage and you'll have a slick, polished edit before you know it.

Step one: Detach Audio Right-click on a clip and select *Detach Audio*. This will show the audio separately underneath the video. Detaching audio allows you to be more precise with starts and stops when doing jump cuts or inserting music.

If you filmed extra audio with a portable mic or recorder, you can select the audio that you've detached from the visual file and delete it.

Step two: Add audio If you recorded audio on a portable device, you'll want to import it. You may also want to pick some music to use alongside your footage.

At the top right of the screen showing your imported video, you'll see a volume diagram. Next to that, there are five small icons of a musical note, a camera, the letter T, an envelope and an image of the world. By selecting the musical note, your whole iTunes library and the music on your computer will be accessible. You can view the names, artists and durations of tracks here, and there is a search bar for easy navigation. To view the audio you recorded on your external device, make sure it's been imported into your iTunes library and isn't sitting on your desktop. If it's in iTunes, you'll be able to see it when you click on the musical note.

Once you've selected the audio you want, click and hold to drag and drop it onto the imported video.

Step three: Cut Now you want to select the good parts in which you didn't mess up, and drag them to the project area at the top left of the iMovie screen. To do this, click on one of the imported clips and a yellow box will come up. Drag the left side of the yellow box to the spot you want your video to start, and the right side of the box to the spot you want the video to end. It doesn't matter about accuracy at this stage as we will use the Split Clip function to create more accurate jump cuts once the clip is in the project window. Go through your entire video, selecting the good bits and dragging them to the project window.

Once the video is in the project window, you can cut out the bad bits more precisely. To split a clip, start by clicking and selecting the movie clip in the timeline that you want to divide. Now move your mouse pointer over the clip to display the skimmer, and skim through the video by moving the mouse pointer left or right. Position the skimmer at the frame in the video where you want to split the clip. Click again to set the play head at that frame. Now navigate to the top screen, and choose *Edit >Split Clip*. Remember that when you're doing jump cuts you should split the clip as close to the sound as possible. Then delete the bits in between that are full of waffle or errors.

Step four: Images and infographics Make sure the image or infographic is imported into iPhoto, then click on the camera icon underneath the preview window, to the right of the musical note icon. This will bring up your iPhoto library. Select the image you want to insert into your video and drag it to the right place in the project window.

Step five: Intro Your set intro will be the same for all your videos, and should be saved on your desktop and in your iMovie Event Library. Open it up and drag it to the start of your project.

Step six: Add transitions in moderation As I explained earlier, I don't recommend using transitions in between every scene as it slows the video down. However, sometimes transitions are useful if you are moving around a lot in the video, as they make the change between settings smoother. It can also be useful to do a fade if you are inserting an image or infographic and you want the move between your presentation and the image to look seamless.

You will find the transitions by clicking on the icon that looks like an envelope, next to the T icon. *Fade to Black*, *Fade to White* and *Cross Blur* are the most useful ones, as transitions like *Swap*, *Cube* and *Mosaic* take up too much time and are too distracting for viewers.

Step seven: Add text Text is useful in two ways. Firstly, it helps bring important points to life to reinforce your message and the theme of your video. Secondly, you need a call to action at the end of your video, and it's a good idea to write the word 'subscribe' over the footage. In Chapter 6, I'll explain how you can make the word 'subscribe' become interactive so that anyone watching your video can click on the word and be taken to a YouTube page where they can subscribe to your channel. This is done using cards and annotations once your video has been uploaded to YouTube.

To add text like 'subscribe' to a video, click on the T icon below the video preview screen. This will bring up a lot of boxes giving you different options of where you want the text to appear on screen. Most vloggers use the Lower option or Gradient White, as the others are too distracting.

Select the text style you like, then click and drag it to the project window while keeping your finger on the mouse. You don't want to let go of it until it's in the correct spot of your video. Navigate to the area where you want the text to appear and hover the mouse over the video until the clip turns blue. If you don't want the text to be over the entire clip, move the mouse back until only part of the clip is blue. Then let go. Your text box should appear above the video clip, and when you preview it you will see if it's in the right place over the visual image.

As a rule, text should be on screen only for between four and eight seconds, as people will stop paying attention after this point. You can check the duration of your text box by double-clicking on it to bring up the Inspector. If necessary, shorten the duration. After doing this you may need to change the position of the text box to get it back in the middle of your clip. To do this, click once to give the text box a yellow-highlighted rim and drag it to the correct position.

To personalise the text, navigate to the video preview screen to the right of the project window. Select the generic text, which is usually 'title text here' and it should turn blue. This enables you to delete 'title text here' and replace it with something like 'subscribe'. In the top right of the video preview screen, you will see a box that says *Show Fonts*. Click on that to personalise your text further by choosing a colour and font to match your brand. You can also make the text bigger or smaller.

Step eight: Music and sound effects This requires the icon that looks like a musical note. Whether you've bought a track or downloaded free music, make sure it is in your iTunes library. This is because clicking on the musical note icon will bring up four folders to look for your audio file: iMovie Sound Effects, iLife Sound Effects, GarageBand and iTunes. You'll make life a lot easier if you can simply open up the iTunes option and scroll down to find the music you need.

After finding the track you want to add as background music, it's time to add it to the video. Click on the song you want. Hold and drag it to your project, and drop it at the start of your movie. Make sure you don't drag it over a clip, because you'll want to adjust the volume of your video and the audio separately, making sure the music adds to the video rather than detracting from what you're saying. You'll know if it's over the clip because it will turn the whole clip green. To avoid this, navigate to the very start of your video.

To add background music to a particular part of a video clip, you can drop the audio over the video. Bear in mind that the audio will run from where it starts to the end of the video clip. If you want it to end earlier than that, select the audio, and while the border turns yellow, drag the slider back to where you want the music to end.

Now you can adjust and edit the background music. I recommend using iMovie's audio-ducking feature. This automatically lowers the background audio so it doesn't compete with your voice. To find the ducking feature, select the audio that you consider your main audio, and click on the Action menu (which looks like a gear). It will bring up three options: *Clip Trimmer*, *Clip Adjustments* and *Audio Adjustments*. Click on *Audio Adjustments* and check the box next to *Ducking*. This should automatically ensure your audio can be heard over the background music. However, if you feel the background music is too quiet, you can click on *Audio Adjustments* again and use the volume slider at the top to test different volume levels.

Step nine: Export movie When you're finished, you need to save your project. Click on *Share* at the top of the iMovie window and scroll down to *Export*. Name your project and choose a size. I recommend clicking on the largest size if possible as it will look better when uploaded to YouTube.

TIP: PAUSING AND FREEZING DURING FILMING MAKES EDITING EASIER

You can simplify the editing process by changing the way you film. These two tactics will make it easier for you to spot where to cut your videos and make the jump-cut process appear smoother.

Pause: Pausing between big ideas or key points will mean that, if you mess up, you don't have to retake the whole video again. It's a lot easier to get small chunks of information right than it is to film a long monologue perfectly, especially as you can look at your video script in between takes. The editing process will also be easier, as you can piece together your small clips rather than waste time searching for the good bits in a long clip.

Freeze: If you do mess up, don't panic. Stop and stay in the same position while you think about what to say next. Don't bash yourself on the head or play with your hair or wriggle on the spot. Simply take a few deep breaths and start again. This will make you look less crazy when it comes to jump-cutting.

WINDOWS MOVIE MAKER

Windows Movie Maker is video-editing software that either comes with your PC or can be downloaded for free. It's enough to handle the basic editing principles if you haven't got a Mac laptop or desktop. If you don't have it already installed, download it from the Microsoft website.

Open Movie Maker and click on *File >New Project*. Choose a name relevant to the subject of your vlog and save it in a place you'll easily find.

You'll notice that the Windows Movie Maker screen is divided into three regions. Along the top is the Ribbon, and this is where editing tools, including transitions, text and audio levels are located. Also on the Ribbon is the Add tool, where you will import video, audio and photos, and the disk icon, which is a quick way to save your work.

The preview window is below the Ribbon on the left, and it's where you can watch your vlog in progress, including in full-screen mode, and rewind or fast-forward to view the sections you're working on.

The timeline window, where you will do your editing, is underneath the Ribbon on the right. Your clips are stored here once they've been imported, and it's here where you can split them, rearrange them into their final order, and add text and audio.

When you look at the jumble of imported clips in the timeline window, it's easy to worry that it will be impossible to produce a slick edited video. However, just take things step by step, and in seven steps you'll have a high-quality video.

Step one: Import video Navigate to the Ribbon and click *Add* *videos and photos.* This will bring up a drop-down box, and you should scroll through it to find the files you wish to upload. Highlight these files and click *Open*. They will be added to your movie's timeline.

Step two: Split clips Play your video sequence and you'll see a black cursor moving through the frames of video. Stop the cursor at the point that you want to split your clip. You can also drag it to the required position.

Now navigate to the *Edit* tab above the Ribbon. When you click on it, you'll see a *Split* button appear. Once the black cursor is in the right place, click on this button and Movie Maker will split the clip into two.

Newer versions of Windows Movie Maker do not allow you to detach the audio, which means you need to be careful when cutting clips. Use the video preview screen on the left to try to cut it as close to the end of your sentence as possible, and to start the next clip close to the start of your first word. However, don't cut out any sound. It's better to have a bit of silence than to cut off part of a word, so err on the side of caution.

Step three: Import audio If you're importing audio from an external device, use the button in the Ribbon called *Add music*. This button allows you to import a wide range of audio file types including wav and mp3.

Where do you want the audio to go? If it's the audio of your speech recorded on an external device, you'll want it at the start of your clip, so make sure the black cursor is there. If you're inserting some music, place the black cursor where you want the music to start.

The audio will appear in a green box above the video footage. You can adjust its length by adjusting the size of the box – click on each end to do this. You can also click and drag the box to make sure it's in the best possible position in relation to the visuals.

Step four: Adjust audio levels The volume of each clip can be adjusted separately. To do this, select a clip, go to *Edit >Video volume* and adjust to the desired level. You may want to adjust the audio of all clips to set them to the same level; alternatively, you may want to make certain parts of your video sound louder or softer to compensate for volume inconsistencies in the recording. Just make sure you've first split the clip you want to adjust. You can also add volume fades by right-clicking on the audio file and selecting *Fade in* or *Fade out*.

If you've added a music track, listen carefully to see how it sounds in relation to your speech. If the music is interfering and overbearing, turn it down by right-clicking the green music file and selecting *Volume*.

If you feel the music file starts too abruptly, then you can make the volume increase gradually. Right-click on the green music file and select *Fade in*.

Finally, make sure that you trim any music tracks you've inserted. In iMovie, the music ends when your video does, but in Movie Maker the audio can go on for long after your video has stopped. Drag the cursor to one or two seconds after your movie ends and split the audio clip. Then delete the last part. To make it even smoother, right-click the music file and select *Fade out*.

Step five: Add transitions Where would you like to place the transition? Windows Movie Maker always inserts transitions at the beginning of clips, so, if you haven't divided your video into clips yet, do that first (step two). Move the black cursor so that the clip you want to add the transition to is in front of it.

Now click on the *Animations* tab above the Ribbon, and you'll see a wide variety of transition choices. Pick one, click on it and it will appear at the start of the clip. If it's not in the right place, click the Undo icon above the Ribbon and try again until the transition is where you want it.

Transitions can last from a quarter of a second up to two seconds. If you feel your transition is too long or short, click the *Duration* box in the Ribbon to adjust it.

Step six: Add text Don't forget to add a call to action to your video! It's a good idea to include the word 'subscribe' at the end of your video, and you may also want to add the URL of your website or blog. To add a line of text to any clip, click on the *Caption* button in the Ribbon of the *Home* tab. This will insert a yellow text box underneath the visual footage in the timeline.

The default text entered is 'enter text here'. To delete that and replace it with what you want to say, you need to be in the video preview screen. Once there, click on 'enter text here' and an editing box will come up around it, allowing you to delete what's there and enter new text. You'll see options in the *Format* tab of the Ribbon for font size and colour. If you want to position the text in the corner rather than the centre, click the text box to highlight it and drag it to a different position. How long do you want the text to stay on screen? Use the *Start time* and *Text duration* buttons in the Ribbon to achieve the desired effect.

Step seven: Save movie You can save your finished vlog to your computer ready for upload by clicking the *Save movie* menu to the right of the Share section in the Ribbon. You can choose from several file formats for your movie, depending on where it will be viewed and on which devices Movie Maker will recommend as a format for your project, so you could use this or experiment with the other settings to make sure you get a high-quality video for upload to YouTube.

TIP: LOOK FOR VIDEO TUTORIALS ON YOUTUBE

If you want to see someone demonstrate Windows Movie Maker, it's a good idea to search YouTube for a video tutorial. I recommend:

LittleWorldofEline (youtube.com/littleworldofeline): Search for the video entitled *How I Edit My Videos with Windows Movie Maker*.

Call Me Rae (youtube.com/callmerae): Search for the video entitled *How to Edit Beauty Videos in Windows Movie Maker*.

Nick's Computer Fix Tutorial (youtube.com/nickscomputerfix): Search for the video entitled *Windows Movie Maker Tutorial – Tips & Tricks & How To's*.

FINAL CUT PRO X AND ADOBE PREMIERE PRO CC

After six months of getting to grips with iMovie or Windows Movie Maker, you should know how to cut a video and add some titles and a couple of basic transitions. At this point, some vloggers feel that it's time to move on to editing software with more features. Apple's Final Cut Pro X (Mac-only) and Adobe Premiere Pro CC (Mac and PC) both have a wealth of features, but they don't come cheap. Final Cut Pro costs £299 and Premiere Pro requires a subscription to Adobe of at least £17 per month.

So what do you get for your money?

GREATER CREATIVE POTENTIAL:

These programmes allow you to work with several layers of video and audio in their timeline sections, making it easier to produce complex professional-looking vlogs. The layering of video means you can create 'picture in picture' effects; for example, you could have a small square of you talking to camera superimposed on footage of the thing you're talking about (such as a computer game, event, prank or shopping trip).

PRECISE EDITING

While in the timeline, you can zoom in and fine-tune your video and audio to the frame or audio sample level, which is very useful for creating jump cuts.

AUDIO-VIDEO SYNC

If you've recorded your audio separately using a portable device, syncing it up to the video footage can be very time-consuming. Thankfully, these programmes both have the ability to automatically sync your audio to your video with just a few clicks, so no one will ever guess you recorded them separately.

COLOUR AND LIGHTING CORRECTION

If your shots are too dark or suffering from an unflattering colour cast such as yellowish artificial light, you have the power to correct this. Sophisticated editing tools allow you to adjust brightness, contrast and colour balance to make your footage more attractive, and they can also be used to add quirky effects.

MORE TRANSITIONS AND EFFECTS

These programmes contain a dizzying amount of choice when it comes to transitions and effects. You can also download more in the form of third-party plugins to increase your options even further.

MORE STYLES OF TEXT

You have a vast choice of fonts and editing tools for customising the look and feel of your titles, captions and calls to action. Your vlogs have a better chance of looking unique if you have more control over how your text looks.

SUPERIOR AUDIO-EDITING CAPABILITIES

Both programmes allow you to manipulate your audio tracks beyond basic volume control – for example, to reduce background noise or add effects and filters. You can mix your audio tracks in mono or stereo, and, if you want to delve further into audio editing, you can even create 5.1 surround sound.

ACCESS TO ONLINE SUPPORT COMMUNITIES AND TUTORIALS

As both programmes are widely used, there are extensive online communities of professional users willing to help out beginners, and a vast library of tutorials available.

If you're intrigued by these programmes but wary of spending money, why not make use of a free trial? Both Adobe and Apple offer free trials for their software on their respective websites, adobe.com/uk and apple.com/uk. That way you can play around with the software and see how you find it. You may find that you prefer iMovie or Windows Movie Maker at the end of the trial, and you've saved yourself some money.

These software packages have so many features, there isn't space in this chapter to do them justice. Also, the type of features you'll end up using will depend on what kind of vlogs you're making. Therefore, look for online tutorials to guide you. Some tutorials give an overview of the basics and some go into detail about specific features and functions. You'll find useful tutorials and helpful tips at the following websites.

LYNDA.COM (LYNDA.COM)

This online education company offers high-quality video courses in Final Cut Pro and Premiere Pro, with tutorials suitable for all ability levels. The site charges a monthly subscription fee to view its videos, but there is an option of a month's free trial. To find the tutorial you need, just use the search browser in the top bar of the homepage.

MACPROVIDEO.COM (MACPROVIDEO.COM)

This online tutorial company provides video courses run by industry professionals on Final Cut Pro and Premiere Pro for a monthly subscription fee.

APPLE SUPPORT (APPLE.COM/UK/SUPPORT)

Apple has made free tutorial videos for Final Cut Pro covering the basics such as importing media, managing libraries and creating 3D titles. The support site also has a community of users to help you find answers to common problems.

ADOBE SUPPORT (HELPX.ADOBE.COM/UK)

The maker of Premiere Pro has a vast library of online video tutorials, suitable for all ability levels and available to watch free of charge.

SHAMELESS MAYA (YOUTUBE.COM/SHAMELESSMAYA)

Shameless Maya has 680,000 YouTube followers and uses Final Cut Pro X to edit all her videos. Search for her video entitled *How I Edit My Videos for YouTube* and you'll see how a professional vlogger uses Final Cut Pro X. It's a very detailed tutorial, starting with how to import video before explaining how to arrange it in the timeline and how to colour-correct and make colours stand out.

CHASEONTWOWHEELS
(YOUTUBE.COM/CHASEONTWOWHEELS)

Chase, a motorcycling vlogger, has 330,000 subscribers on YouTube. He uses Premiere Pro to produce his vlogs and has created an in-depth tutorial video entitled *How I Edit a Vlog [Premiere Pro]*. Among other effects, he demonstrates the 'picture in picture' technique.

These are just a few examples of where to find tutorials for

Final Cut Pro X and Adobe Premiere Pro CC. There are hundreds more out there for you to find and learn from.

OTHER EDITING SOFTWARE

Final Cut Pro and Premiere Pro aren't the only alternatives to Windows Movie Maker and iMovie. Sony produces two video-editing packages, Vegas and Movie Studio: Vegas is aimed towards professional filmmakers and is priced as such (around £390), whereas Movie Studio has fewer features but is cheaper at around £50. You can find more information at sonycreativesoftware.com/vegassoftware.

Avid Media Composer is industry-standard software which was used to edit *Mad Max: Fury Road* and *Sherlock*. However, it's beyond the reach of most people starting out vlogging, as it costs $1,300 or a subscription of at least $35 per month (avid.com/en/media-composer).

A more affordable option could be VideoPad by NCH Software (nchsoftware.com/videopad). The most complete version of the software is the Master's Edition, which is suitable for commercial use and costs $99. There is a free version for home use only, but, as you're planning to make money from your vlogs, this wouldn't be the best choice!

There are even more to choose from. So if you're not convinced by the options so far, search Google for 'video-editing software' to find options for most budgets and comprehensive reviews.

After reading this chapter you should:

☐ Know what a jump cut is and when to use one

☐ Create an introduction that you can use for all of your vlogs

☐ Have a list of websites that will help you create infographics

☐ Be able to search free music websites for an appropriate soundtrack

☐ Be able to import and edit a video in Apple's iMovie

☐ Know how to use Windows Movie Maker to edit a video

☐ Appreciate some benefits of more expensive software such as Final Cut Pro X and Adobe Premiere Pro CC

☐ Know where to go to access free trials and tutorials

CHAPTER 6

YOUTUBE TIPS AND TRICKS

Vlogging and YouTube are irrevocably linked. Without YouTube, vloggers would find it difficult to upload their video journals to the Internet. Without vloggers, YouTube wouldn't receive nearly as much traffic and its advertising revenue would take a significant hit.

YouTube serves three purposes for vloggers. Firstly, it acts as a distribution platform, enabling you to share your content with the world. Before YouTube was founded in 2006, there were video platforms available but none had comparable user numbers. YouTube has more than a billion registered users. Its nearest competitor, Vimeo, is less than one-tenth the size with 100 million registered users. Secondly, YouTube acts as a social network. It allows vloggers to communicate directly with their audience through its comments function, helping the vlogger grow a loyal following. Finally, YouTube acts as a monetisation tool by selling adverts on videos and paying vloggers a commission.

Because YouTube and vlogging are intertwined in these ways, a small shift in the way a vlogger works with YouTube can dramatically alter the number of views their videos receive and the amount of money they earn as a result. If you want to maximise the revenue you earn from YouTube, you need to actively alert YouTube users to your new videos and partner with YouTube to ensure you earn money from adverts. You've worked hard on creating an entertaining video and editing it to a high standard, but that could be for nothing if you don't use YouTube in the best way possible.

There are three crucial steps to take to maximise YouTube revenue. The first is to get your videos seen by as many people as possible. The second is to convert these viewers into subscribers. The last step involves partnering with YouTube and ensuring all the features of your YouTube account are fully enabled.

VIEWERS

Here are some tips to increase the number of views your videos receive.

SMARTEN UP YOUR CHANNEL

First impressions count! If you leave your YouTube page blank without customising the profile picture and banner, people will assume that you don't care about your channel.

Customising your channel is your opportunity to draw people in and set the tone for the videos to come. Choose your colours to match your branding and make sure your logo is in a prominent position.

To add channel art, which is the large rectangular banner you see at the top of vloggers' YouTube channels, sign into YouTube and navigate to My Channel. Near the top of the screen, click *Add channel art*. If your channel already has channel art, just hover on the existing banner until you see the pencil icon, click the icon and select *Edit channel art*. Upload an image from your computer and you'll see a preview of how the art will appear across different devices. To make changes, click *Adjust the crop*. When you're happy, click *Select*. For the best results on all devices, YouTube recommends uploading a single 2560 by 1440 px image.

Don't forget to create an up-to-date channel icon. This will appear as a square image in the upper-left corner of your channel art and will appear every time you leave a comment on someone else's video. Some vloggers like JacksGap display their logo in words, while others like Zoella use their face. YouTube recommends uploading an 800 by 800 px image, which YouTube will resize to 98 by 98 px.

Once you're happy with the general design, think about what content you want to display. Your channel is a shop that viewers are passing by. How do shops entice potential customers to enter? They show off their best products in their windows. In the same way, you need to make sure your best videos are easy to find and the most up-to-date videos are immediately visible.

To keep your channel organised, introduce some playlists. These help to tidy up your virtual shop so the most attractive content is easy to see. They also make it easy for viewers to find exactly what

they're looking for. Some vloggers organise playlists by format –
e.g. daily vlogs, hauls and reactions – while others organise theirs
by subject – e.g. hair, make-up and body creams. You only need
three to four playlists to show off the content you're most proud
of. Everything else can go in the Recent uploads section.

Shops don't have any control over the packaging of the
products they stock on their shelves, but you can change the way
you display your videos on YouTube. Every time you upload a
video, YouTube allows you to select a still as the thumbnail. This
is the image that shows up on your channel to entice people to
watch the video. Make sure it sums up what the video is about!

BE CAREFUL WITH TITLE AND VIDEO DESCRIPTIONS

YouTube users find videos by searching for the topics they're
interested in. The titles of your videos need to contain words
related to the subjects you've covered if they're to come up in
search results. You might have made a fantastic beauty blog about
how to achieve Kylie Jenner's full lips using lipliner, but if you call
your video something vague like 'lip magic', the video won't be
seen by anyone searching for 'Kylie Jenner' or 'lipliner tutorial'.

When thinking of a title, make sure that the very first word is
a keyword that's relevant to the contents of the video. You should
follow that with the main feature of the video. To use the previous
example, a video explaining how to achieve Kylie Jenner's lips
should be entitled *Kylie Jenner Make-Up: Lipliner Tutorial*. The
first word – 'Kylie' – generates thousands of search requests every
day. Including the words 'make-up' and 'tutorial' in the title will
mean that the video comes up in search results for those terms too.

Be aware that some keywords are searched-for more than others. Most of you will be familiar with the mass appeal of cute animal videos. Because of this, vloggers have been known to include the name of an animal in their title just so it will come up in searches. I don't recommend this, as viewers who feel conned won't return. If your video is related to make-up, then you need to use make-up terms in the title. But did you know that 'eye make-up' is searched-for more than 'eyeliner', or that 'make-up tutorial' is searched-for more than 'make-up' alone?

Google's Keyword Tool allows you to see search statistics so you can pick the most popular terms for your title. To access it, type adwords.google.com into your web browser and then register for an account. Once you're registered, you'll be taken to a home screen and see several options in tabs on the top bar. Click on *Tools* and scroll down to *Keyword Planner*. This will bring up a complicated-looking search box. Don't worry about anything but the Product or Service area. In this area, write down the term you want to research, scroll down the page and click *Get Ideas*.

For example, enter the word 'lipliner' and you will see that 'best lipliner' is searched-for more often than 'lipliner'. However, both pale into comparison next to 'lip make-up', which is searched-for twice as much as 'lipliner' and 'best lipliner'. Based on this information, we would change our title to *Kylie Jenner Beauty Tutorial: Lip Make-up*, as lip make-up is searched-for more often than lipliner.

Now check whether 'Kylie Jenner' is more searched-for than 'lip make-up'. If it is, keep 'Kylie' as the first word of the title; if not, swap it around so the most searched-for term is first. In this case, 'Kylie Jenner' generates millions of searches, which is significantly more than 'lip make-up'.

Now check that the first fifty-five characters of the title make sense. Although you can use up to a hundred characters, search results only show the first fifty-five to sixty characters. This is why it's best to put the most important and compelling words at the start of your title.

Once you've figured out your title, you should take similar care over what you enter in the description box of your video. Search engines also refer to video descriptions to decide whether a video is relevant to a particular search term, so make sure your description contains every keyword you can think of. There's no need to be succinct or conservative with your video description, and you should aim to write more rather than less to ensure you've included everything that could be searched-for.

However, it is advisable to put the most useful information at the top of the description box. YouTube displays only a small teaser of text, and viewers have to click *Read more* if they want to see the full description. That teaser text consists of 157 characters, and should be a mix of keywords and URLs. Many vloggers link to a previous video they've made on a similar subject to encourage viewers to watch their other videos. The more videos people watch, the higher the Average Watch Time of your channel. You need to work hard to grow this figure, as YouTube uses it to determine how high up your videos come in a list of search results. For example, if there were five vloggers who had all made Kylie Jenner lipliner tutorials and given them similar titles, the one that would come at the top of the search list would be the one whose channel had the highest Average Watch Time.

If your landing-page URL is very long or doesn't contain any relevant keywords, consider using a URL shortener like bit.ly to customise the link. Both Zoella and PointlessBlog often use this tactic, as it means they can make more use of the 157 characters.

For the rest of the description, be as keyword-rich as possible. A good rule of thumb is to write 200–500 words to create context and value for the viewer and to include as much relevant text as possible that could help people find you when searching. The more YouTube knows about your video via your title, tags and description, the more confidence they will have to rank it. Make sure the description content is unique and not copied from another blog or article that you've written about the subject. YouTube frowns on duplicated content, so this will harm your Search Engine Optimisation (SEO).

You should also include more URLs throughout your content if you want to direct people to your blog, website, Facebook or Twitter. YouTube allows you to insert hyperlinks so viewers can click on the links and visit the website straight away. At the end of the description, have a link for viewers to subscribe to your channel. The most successful vloggers – the ones that are rich – have all done this. Check out any of their videos and you'll see lots of links in the description box.

TIP: SCHEDULE VIDEOS

Never set your video to publish straight away. You want to have time to optimise your title and think about your description. Set your video to private, make sure the title and description sum up what your video is about and that you've included appropriate keywords, and then publish it at a time when you know most of your viewers will be online. If you're aiming at young people in the UK, you don't want to publish a video at 7am as all your audience will be in bed!

POST REGULARLY

The most successful vloggers upload content at least three times a week, and often once a day. Vlogger KSI has more subscribers than anyone else in the UK, 12 million, and he uploads one video a day. Viewers have an insatiable appetite for new material, and the more content you can give them, the more they'll keep coming back.

When you start vlogging, it will take more time for you to film and edit videos, so you may prefer to aim for one or two uploads a week. This is fine as long as you can be consistent. It's better to do fewer videos and be consistent than post five times one week and zero another week.

If your viewers learn that you post a video every Tuesday and Thursday, for example, they will get into the habit of coming back and checking for new videos on those days. Let them down and you risk losing them altogether. It takes twenty-one days to build a habit, but one day to break it. Once you fail to put something up on the designated day, your viewers will stop returning on that day. Instead, they'll check back every few weeks and some will visit only every few months. This will put a significant dent in your regular viewership.

Committing to a regular vlogging schedule is important not only for your audience, but it's a great way to keep yourself motivated. If you've set yourself a goal to upload new content every Tuesday and Thursday, you will work hard to get it done so that you don't disappoint anyone. Without that deadline, it's easier to put off the work. Before you know it, you're uploading only once a week, and then once every two weeks, because you don't have the same pressure.

Have a holiday coming up? You could always film two videos at once – with a change of outfits in between – and use YouTube's scheduling feature to ensure your content goes up on its usual day. It's very easy to do. Every time you upload a video, you'll see a Privacy Settings box, which has four options – *Public*, *Unlisted*, *Private* and *Scheduled*. Check the *Scheduled* option and choose a date and time.

If you're new to YouTube and not yet Partner-verified, you need to follow one additional step as YouTube only lets its partners schedule videos. To check whether you are verified or not, navigate to your channel and click on the circle icon in the very top-right corner of the screen. This will bring up a box where you can select *Creator Studio*. Once in Creator Studio mode, click on the left sidebar entry *Channel*, then *Status and features*. If your channel is verified and YouTube considers you a partner, your Account status will say 'Partner verified'. If it isn't, you'll see a button marked *Verify* next to the name of your channel. Click this and follow the steps outlined. As soon as you've done this, the Privacy Settings box will give you the *Scheduled* option next time you upload a video.

What days or times should you pick when scheduling video? Frederator Networks runs over 1,300 different YouTube channels and generates around 120 million views every month. After analysing every one of its uploads and gathering as much data as possible, the company found that posting videos on the following days and times resulted in more viewers: Monday to Wednesday at 2–4pm, Thursday and Friday at 12–3pm, Saturday and Sunday at 9–11am. They also found that Thursday, Friday and Saturday were the best days to post in general. However, bear in mind that timing makes a tiny difference. Quality of content is more important than timing. Once you start getting a reputation for posting high-quality videos that entertain and educate, people will come back and find you at the time you choose.

Joe Penna has 2.8 million subscribers to his YouTube channel MysteryGuitarMan (youtube.com/MysteryGuitarMan). He is a big fan of sticking to a regular schedule when releasing videos, and says: 'It's really important to stick to a schedule, because sometimes YouTube messes up their subscription box and people who are subscribed to you don't get your videos. So if people are coming back every Tuesday, every Thursday or every day then you get that *real* audience.'

BE ACTIVE IN THE COMMUNITY

YouTube consists of thousands of communities of people who share common interests. Each community can consist of millions of people. When you join a community and play an active role in it, you widen your reach. Every time you leave a useful comment under another vlogger's video, others in the community might click on your profile picture to find out more about you and be intrigued enough to watch one of your videos. The more comments you leave, the more your traffic will grow.

Also, make sure you acknowledge people who have commented on your videos. Reply to their comments and check out their YouTube channels. Revisit the comments section several times throughout the week after each upload so you can respond to viewers who were late to the party. Responding to comments keeps viewers feeling appreciated and valued, and they're more likely to return as a result.

VIDEO RESPONSES

Instead of leaving a comment under another vlogger's video, you could create a video response. This is relatively easy to do, and could lead to a substantial number of new visitors to your channel if you create a succinct response to a popular video. To find the most popular video that's relevant to your subject, enter your subject niche in the YouTube search box and scroll down to see what's popular.

Select the videos with the most views and you'll notice that next to the comment box you can click *Create a video response*. This will direct you to a page listing all the videos you've ever uploaded to YouTube. If you're making a special response, then you need to film it and upload it to YouTube to see it in the search results. Then simply select the video you'd like to use as your video response. Responding to the right video can get you as many as 1,000 extra views.

COLLABORATE

When you collaborate with another vlogger, your videos will be seen by their audience. So if you collaborate with someone with thousands of viewers, it could bring a huge traffic boost to your channel. To find out how to identify potential collaborators and approach them, see Chapter 8.

USE CARDS

Cards are interactive annotations that allow vloggers to add links to associated websites or related videos. You can set them to pop up at any time during the video and they will appear on screen in a small teaser box. If a viewer clicks on the box, they will see your link to a related video or external website.

Cards replace YouTube's annotations feature, which had the same functionality but only worked on desktop devices. As more than 50 per cent of content is now being viewed on mobile devices, cards are a way of making sure your annotations reach everyone.

Look carefully and you'll see that the big names on YouTube fill their videos with cards linking to their other content. Why is this? It's because interlinking videos is one of the best ways to increase visibility. Think about it. You have a YouTube account full of videos that you've created. Someone happens to run a particular search query on Google and ends up clicking a link to your video. At this point, they're already watching your content, so why not throw in a card in the bottom corner that takes them to another one of your videos? Now you've converted one view into two views. This will increase the Average Watch Time of your channel, which will increase your search engine visibility. Interlinking creates a web of content that sucks viewers right in. You will lose out on a lot of potential views if you don't utilise it.

To create a card, follow these five steps:

- Sign into your YouTube Video Manager, find the video you want to add cards to and click *Edit*.
- Click on the *Cards* button in the top navigation bar.
- Click on *Add card* to open up the creation window for the card type you want to add. Enter a valid URL applicable to that card type.
- Upload an image (or pick one from the suggestions offered). Edit and optimise the title and call-to-action text.
- Click *Create card*, and if required, adjust the time you want it to appear.

YouTube allows vloggers to add up to five cards per video. If you want to change the content on a card, you can edit it at any time. Simply select the video you want to edit, tick the *Edit* box next to it, find the *Cards* tab and click *Edit* next to the card you want to change. Cards can also be deleted.

EVALUATE AND ADJUST

YouTube can provide you with a lot of useful statistics related to your audience and the average viewing time for your videos. Access this by signing in to your YouTube account and typing 'youtube.com/analytics' into your web browser.

The data you see includes reports on how people find your

videos, how long they watch them for and on what devices they watch – mobile, tablet or desktop.

If people find your videos from a certain source more than others, you know to spend more time engaging with that outlet. This outlet could be a social media network or it could be through your blog or website. You should also question why your other efforts aren't working and change your strategy slightly.

Are people watching your videos until the end? If not, it's a sign that you need to make your videos more engaging. Ask people who have commented on your videos what would make them watch more of your work.

SUBSCRIBERS

Once you've applied some of the tactics above to grow the number of views your videos receive, you need to think about how you can turn viewers into subscribers. Businesses and marketing agencies value subscribers over video views when deciding whether to work with vloggers. This is because subscribing to a channel indicates a person is loyal to and influenced by that channel. Also, it is a consistent figure. Some of your videos may have had hundreds of views and some may have reached tens or hundreds of thousands, but the number of subscribers is more constant.

Every viewer is a potential subscriber, so you may assume all you need to do to convert them is to ask people to subscribe and tell them how to do it. Sadly, it's not as easy as that. In fact, begging for subscribers will not only have the opposite effect and repel viewers from clicking the button to subscribe, but it could put them off watching your videos altogether. Imagine if you were in a pub or a bar and went round the room asking people to be your friend. Most people would think you were weird, and it's highly unlikely you'd end up with any friends. However, if you got chatting to a group of people, had a fun and interesting conversation, stopped before they got bored and moved on to another group, you'd have people queuing up to be your friends. YouTube works in a similar way. You need to make people want to subscribe.

Think carefully about what viewers get out of your videos that nobody else can offer them. Go back to the notes and plans you made for your YouTube channel if necessary – you should have written down what sets your channel apart from the rest. This might be beauty videos that help viewers look as glamorous as celebrities, it might be fashion videos that always tell you what's new on the high street or it may be reviews of computer games with cheats and tips to help viewers complete the game. Whatever it is, you need to mention it when you ask people to subscribe.

When asking for subscribers, your call to action should consist of three elements – telling viewers what to do (i.e. subscribe), how to do it (by clicking on the button) and why to do it (because you can give them things nobody else can and therefore improve their lives).

For example, a good call to action for a beauty vlogger would be: 'To stay up to date with my videos looking at the freshest, hottest celebrity make-up looks that are fashionable right now, make sure to subscribe to my channel by clicking the box above this video.'

Annotations will also help you turn viewers into subscribers, without the need to beg. Annotations only work on desktop devices, but as there are currently no cards that allow you to link to a *Subscribe* button, reaching 50 per cent of viewers via annotations is better than reaching none at all. There are two ways you should use annotations in your videos. The first is a speech-bubble annotation, which can be added to the video directly under the *Subscribe* button. The edge of the speech bubble looks like an arrow, so it directs viewers to click on the button. You could add this speech bubble midway through the video when you're showing a useful tip or covering an important subject, to impress upon viewers what you're saying. Impressed viewers are more likely to subscribe. The optimal time to have the speech bubble on display is five seconds. Any shorter and it will disappear before people have had chance to click on it; any longer and it will detract from what you're talking about in your video.

The other annotation you can use is a spotlight annotation. This acts like a spotlight over a piece of text on screen, and when viewers hover their mouse over it they will see a box that they can click on to subscribe to your channel. For this to work, you need to have written some text like 'subscribe' over your video during the editing process, before you upload it to YouTube. If you've done that, add a spotlight annotation by navigating to your video manager and checking *Edit* next to the video that requires the annotation. Play the video until you see the word 'subscribe', then hit *Pause*. Navigate to the *Annotations* tab and insert a spotlight annotation box. Drag to move it over the text 'subscribe'. You'll see a box entitled *Link*, and if you check that box it will bring up a drop-down box with *Video* at the top. Scroll down until you see

Subscribe. Select *Subscribe* and you're done. Test it out by playing the video back and clicking on 'subscribe' when it appears on the video screen.

Vloggers with lots of subscribers tend to have 'end cards' to finish each video. End cards usually last 10–15 seconds, and are right at the end of your video, after you've stopped talking. They typically contain links to some of your other videos along with your social media information and another call to subscribe. If you're not including an end card at the end of each video edit, design something now. You may notice an increase in subscribers from the very first time you add an end card.

It's very important to make the end card visually attractive. Don't try to cram in a lot of information. Keeping it simple and clear will be more beneficial in the long term, as it will be easier for a viewer to find a video and click on it. Aim for quality over quantity, and make sure the video preview or still image directing viewers to your previous video is enticing. You want to intrigue viewers so they click on the image or preview to watch the whole video.

TIP: FIND AN END CARD TEMPLATE ONLINE

The simplest way to create a YouTube end card is to make use of free software available online. FullScreen (fullscreen. com) has designed a simple and clear end-screen template in jpeg and Photoshop formats, which can be downloaded from the FullScreen website. Find it by doing a Google search and entering the terms 'Fullscreen.com' and 'end screen'.

If you want to design your own end screen, I recommend using PicMonkey (picmonkey.com). This is a simplified version of Photoshop that's free to use. Simply visit picmonkey.com and choose the option *Design*. This will give you a blank canvas that you can customise with colours relevant to your brand, as well as boxes that will eventually host preview images or video.

The first thing you should do to the canvas in Picmonkey is resize to 1280 by 720 px as this will fit the YouTube screen. If you start with any other size, bits of the end screen you've carefully created will appear stretched or cut off when you insert it into your video. Next choose a background colour and hit *Apply*. Now you're ready to create frames for video previews. Click on the butterfly image to the side of the canvas, which stands for Overlays. Scroll down to the Scrapbook section and you'll see *Labels*. Click on that and choose a basic shape for your video previews.

Now upload your logo to your canvas using the Overlays function. Click on the *Your Own* box at the top of the Overlays menu and upload your logo. It's also a good idea to upload a 'subscribe' call to action as an overlay. Find the YouTube Subscribe logo in Google Images and save it to your desktop. To add it, click on the *Your Own* box again.

If this sounds confusing and you want to see a demonstration, vlogger Carrisa from Makeup By Carrisa has a step-by-step tutorial of how to create an end card using Picmonkey. Search for it on her YouTube channel youtube.com/makeupbycarrisa.

Once you've created an end screen, import it into your video-editing software. If you're using iMovie it will automatically zoom in and out to make the screen appear animated, and you don't want this, so adjust it using the *Adjust* button at the top of the preview screen. Find the cropping tool that looks like a loose box made up of two L shapes and select *Fit* rather than *Crop to fit*. Then alter the duration of the image window so it lasts for ten seconds, and save your project.

The next step is to fill the empty preview boxes with video or images. Video looks more impressive! If using iMovie, scroll down through your Event Library and find the video you want to link to. You only need ten seconds of it, so select the best ten seconds and save it as a separate Event.

With the end screen in your project area, click on the ten-second clip in the Event Library and drag it to the same place. Let go when the red pointer is in the middle of the end screen and you will see a box of options. Click on the picture in *Picture* option and your video should go above the end-screen box. Select it until a thick yellow line develops around the outside of the video and move it so it lines up exactly with where the end screen starts and finishes.

How does it look in the preview window? You'll probably need to alter the size and position of the video clip so it fits in the end screen's preview box. To do this, make sure the video in the project area is selected, with a bold yellow line around it. This will mean that it has arrows around it when it's on the preview screen. Using those arrows, you can resize the video so it fits the frames in your end-screen template and drag the video to the right position. Repeat this process until you've inserted video into all your preview frames.

Every time you upload a video that has an end card to YouTube, you need to add annotations and cards over the end card to fully utilise it. Otherwise viewers will just see the video preview and have no way of watching the full video. Start with annotations, by using spotlight annotations over each video preview box, checking the link box and selecting *Video >Channel Trailer*. Do the same for the *Subscribe* box by using a spotlight annotation to highlight the 'subscribe' text. For cards, it doesn't work well if you have two cards in the same timeframe, so opt for the 'subscribe' card as that's the most important. Set the card to pop up when the end screen comes up, and allow it to last for the whole ten seconds. End cards make your videos look much more professional and provide a clear signpost directing viewers to subscribe. As I said, you should see a difference the first time you use one.

You will also see a big difference in subscriber numbers if you make a channel trailer for your YouTube channel. Channel trailers show up when non-subscribers click on your channel, and play automatically. Once someone subscribes to your channel, they'll no longer see this trailer, as YouTube understands that your subscribers already know what your best content is.

Zoella has a good channel trailer. Visit youtube.com/zoella, remembering to sign out of your YouTube and Google accounts first if you're already a subscriber. The channel trailer will play automatically. Notice that the trailer is just a minute long and contains the best clips of all her videos, featuring lots of happy faces, bright settings, loud laughs and exclamations.

Before you create your own channel trailer, have a look at some of the trailers made by the well-known vloggers I listed in the

Introduction of this book. Remember that their trailers will be visible only if you're not a subscriber: sign out of your YouTube account if you are.

As a general rule, think of your channel trailer as a film trailer, showcasing your best bits so that people will be curious and want to see more.

TIP: MAKE YOUR CHANNEL TRAILER ACTION-PACKED

The following guidelines will help you make a great channel trailer.

DO something quirky, cool or attention-grabbing in the first few seconds, as you want to hook people in and keep their attention for the whole trailer. By default, ads won't appear when the trailer is playing on the channel page in the trailer spot. This helps keep the user focused on learning about and subscribing to your channel.

SHOW, don't tell. Entertain viewers and give them examples of your content, rather than making a new video and talking about what you do. If you're an extreme-sports vlogger, incorporate a crazy trick into your video. If you're a comedy vlogger, make it funny and if you're a beauty vlogger show off some dramatic 'before' and 'after' transformations. Give lots of examples of your best content.

CALL viewers to subscribe! Have a clear call to action in the channel trailer, scripted and annotated as you show fabulous content, giving a reason why people should subscribe. Also, have a link to subscribe in the channel trailer description. Ultimately, the goal of a trailer is to reach non-subscribers, grab them and get them to subscribe, so you have to explain to them how to do it.

SHARE your uploading schedule with viewers, so they feel confident it's worth subscribing to get fresh content regularly. However, don't be too obvious in the video. Hint at it by showing dates, then be more open in your video description.

REVEAL to your viewers *why* you do what you do, not just what you do. For example, beauty vloggers could explain that they enjoy looking good and want others to look and feel good too. Computer-games vloggers might say that they hate feeling frustrated with poor-quality games or tricky stages, and want to share tips to make gaming better for everyone. This needs to be done subtly, because our goal is to show, not tell. But one short sentence revealing your deeper motivation within a trailer that's packed with examples of your best work won't bore the viewer; instead it will make them empathise with you. If you show you're passionate about what you do, people are more likely to get on board and subscribe. Sometimes, they might not even be that interested in what you do – if they're really on board with why you're doing it, sometimes they will subscribe to you anyway.

When you've made a channel trailer, you need to upload it to YouTube and set it as the default trailer seen by new visitors. To do this, follow these steps:

- Upload the video that you want to be your channel trailer.
- Go to My Channel on the YouTube homepage.
- Click on the *For new visitors* tab, which you will see directly above the *What to watch next* video and below the *Home*, *Videos*, *Playlists*, *Channels*, *Discussion* and *About* tabs.
- Click on *Channel trailer*.
- Choose the video by selecting its thumbnail or entering the YouTube URL.

Using social media in the right way will also help you to convert viewers into subscribers. When promoting YouTube on social media, it's easy to share a link to a video to increase video views. But did you know there's a link to your YouTube page that also gives people a Subscribe pop-up? When people click on the link, they're taken to your YouTube channel but they can't view it without subscribing or closing the Subcribe window. You should regularly be sharing this link with your social media networks and incorporating it into your email signatures so that it's reaching as many people as possible. The URL of the link is:

youtube.com/subscription_center?add_user=[insert   your username here]

Remember that you can shorten this link using a URL-shortening tool like bit.ly, which also enables you to see how many people have clicked through. More about bit.ly and other social media tools will be covered in Chapter 7, where I'll also explain ways to grow your social media networks and reach more people.

TIP: MAKE YOUR VIEWERS FEEL USEFUL

To avoid looking desperate when plugging your subscription link on social media, treat it like a game. Set yourself a target subscriber number and tell your social media followers that you *need* them to help you hit your target. For example, if your goal is to get to 1,000 subscribers, tell people this and suggest you will do something quirky or unique when you get to 1,000. People like to know that their subscription makes a difference, and the more attention-grabbing you can make your reward, the better!

YOUTUBE CHANNEL OPTMISATION

Now we've worked on increasing viewing figures and subscriber numbers, the final step is to make sure you can monetise these figures through your YouTube account.

Do you know if all the features of your YouTube channel are enabled? It would be easy to get by using YouTube's basic features, without ever knowing that more is available to help you make money.

YouTube doesn't automatically give you ad revenue, for example. To start receiving it, you must first enable monetisation on your YouTube channel. This is how to do it:

Step 1: Log in to your YouTube account and access your Creator Studio by clicking on your profile icon circle at the top right of the YouTube page.

Step 2: Click on the *Channel* tab in the sidebar and navigate to *Status and features*.

Step 3: Scroll down to the *Monetisation* line and click the *Enable* box.

Step 4: Follow YouTube's steps to enable your account, including agreeing to the terms and conditions and selecting the type of ads you'll allow YouTube to use before or during your videos.

Step 5: Now your account is set up for monetisation in principle, but you won't see any results yet as you need to physically indicate which videos you want to monetise.

To do this, go back to the Creator Studio area and select *Video Manager* from the left sidebar.

Step 6: Click *Edit* next to the video you want to monetise.

Step 7: Underneath the video preview you'll see tabs saying *Basic info*, *Translations*, *Monetisation* and *Advanced settings*. Click the *Monetisation* tab.

Step 8: Choose the type of ads you want to show and click *Save*. I recommend checking every box.

In order to receive payment, you must link your YouTube account with your Google AdSense account. Have you noticed that there's no way to enter your bank details into your YouTube account? That's because YouTube pays you through Google. You should follow these steps to link a YouTube account with a Google AdSense account:

Step 1: Go to the Monetisation page. Get there by clicking your icon in the top right to get into your Creator Studio. Then, in the left menu, click *Channel >Monetisation*.

Step 2: Go to the *How will I be paid?* section.

Step 3: From the AdSense Association page, follow the next step to be directed to AdSense.

Step 4: At the bottom of the page, select the option *Yes* if you already have an AdSense account. You will be directed to sign into your AdSense account by entering your email address and password. If you don't have an AdSense account, follow the steps to sign up for one.

Step 5: Once your account is activated, you'll see a message to inform you that your AdSense application has been received, if you didn't have one already, or a message to say your existing AdSense account has been associated with your YouTube account. Note that it may take up to forty-eight hours for the association to be fully active. Also, new AdSense applicants will receive a letter through the post to confirm their new AdSense account and AdSense ID.

Once you've enabled Monetisation, go back to your Creator Studio to see what else needs to be enabled. In the left sidebar, click on *Channel >Status and features*. Green circles are good, meaning that you have access to that specific feature. Grey circles, on the other hand, indicate features that work for other people but not for you – yet.

You should enable the ability to link annotations to external sites and merchandise partners, as this could make you money. Direct your viewers to a merchandise website, for example, and you'll make money through sales. To do this, look for the Account Status heading at the top of the Status and Features page. Under this heading, you should see a box saying *Verify*. Simply click on *Verify* and follow the steps to validate your phone number. This makes Google confident you're a real person and not a robot, and allows you to make use of External annotations. The circle next to External annotations will turn from grey to green.

If you want to link an annotation to your blog, then one extra step is involved. Is it worth taking this extra step? If you want more money, it is. You can make money through blog-advertising if you direct traffic to your blog. You could also have an online shop on your blog, selling t-shirts or other merchandise. Or you could design a shopfront containing products that link to stores with which you have affiliate deals. I explain more about the benefits of blogging and affiliate deals in Chapter 12. To put it simply, being an affiliate means you receive a percentage each time you direct a viewer to an online store and it results in a sale. The more traffic your blog gets, the more affiliate revenue you're likely to earn. This is why it's in your best interests to direct vlog traffic to your blog.

The extra step you need to take isn't complicated. You just need to register the blog as an associated website and then YouTube will let you link to it. YouTube only lets you link to websites that you've registered as associated, as they need proof that you own that blog or website.

To add your blog as an associated website in your YouTube account, follow these steps:

Step 1: Go to Advanced Channel Settings by clicking *Your account >Creator Studio >Channel >Advanced*.

Step 2: In the *Associated website* section, enter the URL. It will show as pending unless you've verified the site before.

Step 3: Under the URL box, click *Verify* if you own the website, or *Request approval* to have the website's owner approve it. This will take you to Google's Search Console.

Step 4: In Search Console, make sure that you're logged in with the same Google Account as your YouTube channel. If you're unsure, you can check your account information on YouTube.

Step 5: Follow the instructions on screen to add a site to Search Console. You may be asked to choose a verification method.

Step 6: When you've added your site to Search Console, it will go through a verification process. Once verification is complete, the website's status will change from Pending to Success and you'll be able to use an annotation or card to link people to your blog.

When adding an annotation, check the link box and enter the URL of the store on your blog. Then click *Video* to bring up the drop-down menu. Scroll down until you see *Associated website*, select that and save. When adding a card, click *Add card*, scroll down to *Link* and click on the *Create* button next to it. Under *Associated website*, select your website's URL from the *Select site* drop-down menu. Choose the call-to-action and teaser text and click *Create card*.

Another way to sell things and make money is to create an online shop using Shopify (shopify.co.uk) or Etsy (etsy.com). Shopify is a complete ecommerce solution that allows you to set up an online store to sell your goods. You can customise the design of your online shop, take credit-card payments and track and respond to orders for a monthly subscription fee. Shopify is useful if you have a lot of products to sell – things like t-shirts that you've printed in bulk or hats that you've customised with your logo. Etsy is a place where you can sell handmade items, and is good if you're selling a small amount of high-quality or custom-made products. Once your account is enabled, you will be able to link to your store on Shopify or Etsy easily by adding an annotation in the usual way, checking the *Link* box to add a retail URL and choosing the *Merch* category in the drop-down menu.

Music vloggers can also benefit massively from the External annotations feature, as enabling it allows you to link to iTunes, where you can sell your tracks. Or you could link to Ticketmaster, where people can buy tickets to your gigs, helping you to fill out venues and make money. Ticketmaster and iTunes work in the same way as Etsy and Shopify – you need the *Merch* category in the drop-down menu.

Go back to your *Status and features* tab and you'll notice a *Paid content* circle. This feature enables you to monetise your channel by setting a fee that viewers have to pay in order to watch your videos. You get to set the price and put the value on your videos, so in theory you'll make a lot more money than waiting for the commission from YouTube ad sales. However, 'in theory' is the key point here, as Paid content does not work in practice. When viewers can access lots of YouTube channels for free, there is no way they'd pay extra to watch yours unless you have a massive following already. By massive, I mean a fan base as large as the Kardashians, who are just about able to launch paid-for apps using their loyal followers – but only just.

Once you've enabled the monetisation tool and the ability to link to external websites, you can be confident that your channel has all the features you need to make money.

YouTube has made several vloggers seven-figure sums.

CASE STUDY: ROBERT KYNCL, YOUTUBE CBO

Robert Kyncl is the Chief Business Officer at YouTube, where he oversees all business functions including content, sales, marketing, platforms, access and strategy. He gave a speech at the CES conference in January 2016, which included observations of vloggers who'd made money through YouTube, and predicted how YouTube would grow further over the coming decade. Robert said: 'I addressed CES in 2012, when I mentioned the vlogger Michelle Phan and said she would be very successful and wealthy. In 2012, she had 2 million subscribers and four years later she has 7 million. She has her own make-up brand made by L'Oréal, and she's raised $100,000 for her start-up beauty subscription service, Ipsy, which puts the value of her company at $500,000 – half a million! She's certainly doing well!

'YouTube collaborated with the data company Nielsen to gather some statistics about people's viewing habits. We found that between 2015 and 2016, the number of eighteen to thirty-four-year-olds watching TV fell by 9 per cent. However, the number of eighteen to thirty-four-year-olds watching videos online grew by 48 per cent, with mobile viewing making up the largest source of that growth. The data found that the average daily amount of time people spent on their mobile devices consuming videos was 40 minutes – a 50 per cent growth on the year before.

'YouTube is a democratic platform, so success is open to everyone. Everyone can make content about things that interest them and everyone can use YouTube to search for things that interest them. There's everything from make-up and beauty tutorials to computer game walkthroughs and competitions. For that reason, it's a lot more attainable to aim to be the next PewDiePie than it is to try and be the next Tom Cruise.'

Before we end this chapter, let's discuss setting targets. How many YouTube viewers and subscribers do you need to make good money? There are lots of figures waved around, saying that YouTube pays £1 per 1,000 views or £5 per 1,000 views, but it's more complicated than that. YouTube pays based on viewers' engagement with the ads. Engagement means clicking an ad or viewing a promotion for over thirty seconds. You might get a million views but if nobody watches or snaps the advertisements, then you don't profit.

The way to ensure more people watch your ads is to build up a loyal following in a certain niche, so the ads are based on keywords relevant to your video and therefore not annoying to viewers. Statistically speaking, the more viewers and subscribers you have, the more likely it is that some of them will be engaged with the ads. Because of ad-blocking software and issues with ads on mobile devices, approximately 15 per cent of your viewers are actually engaging with an ad. If you have 1,000 viewers, you're only engaging 150 people, whereas if you have a million viewers you may be engaging 150,000 people.

After this, YouTube takes a 45 per cent slice of advertising revenue, so the money you receive dwindles even further. YouTube charges advertisers different amounts for CPM (cost per thousand views), so at the start you may be making anything from £0.20 to £1.50 CPM, but when you get bigger you could be earning close to £6 CPM. For example, let's look at the channel StandUpBits, which was set up by comedians Josef Holm and Claude Shires in 2013. The guys had access to a large library of more than 3,500 stand-up comedy clips that had never been broadcast elsewhere. Once they published these exclusive clips on their channel, they reached a million views within two weeks. They said this meant they earned £1,400. Doing the maths, this means they were making a CPM of £1.40.

The way to reach higher CPM figures is to grow your channel until you are considered for Google's Preferred Content scheme. How do you get on this? It's a case of 'Don't contact us; we'll contact you.' Google will approach you when they have crunched the figures and worked out that you are influential enough to be on the list. To be featured on the Google Preferred Content list, you need to be in the top 5 per cent of YouTube channels that have the highest levels of audience engagement. To work this out, Google uses a special algorithm to give every YouTube channel a preference score. The algorithm takes into account watch time, comments, shares and social embeds.

Once on the list, marketers are more likely to contact you, and you'll receive higher ad revenue as brands pay a premium for advertising on channels proven to be engaging. Another advantage is that YouTube is more likely to promote your vlog and use you in ad campaigns, getting you even more views and subscribers. You can check out the list of vloggers that have made it onto the Preferred Content list at youtube.com/yt/lineups.

Making money from YouTube is a long-term game. Focus on attracting more viewers and growing your subscriber numbers, and the YouTube revenue will come. You can also use your viewers and subscribers to make money through other revenue streams, which I explore in Chapter 9 onwards.

After working through this chapter, you should have:

☐ Customised your YouTube channel with channel art and a channel icon
☐ Used Google's Keywords tool to help you optimise video titles
☐ Understood the importance of posting regularly
☐ Experimented with cards and annotations
☐ Designed an end card template
☐ Created a channel trailer
☐ Verified your YouTube account
☐ Enabled monetisation on your YouTube account and on individual videos
☐ Registered your blog or online store as an associated website

CHAPTER 7

SOCIAL MEDIA STRATEGY

To grow your YouTube channel, you need to tell people it exists. Most of us already have more fans, followers and friends on social media than we do in real life, so it makes sense to use social networks to communicate that you have a channel, that you've uploaded new content and that you're confident viewers will like what they see.

Take a look at the Twitter and Instagram accounts of your favourite vloggers and you'll see their feed is full of links to their latest uploads and responses to viewers' questions about what they were wearing or doing in those videos. Social networks are a great way to have conversations with your viewers so that they feel more like friends – and remain loyal to you because you interact with them.

However, the success with which you can use social media

depends on how many followers you have. Zoella has over 4 million Twitter followers, Joe Sugg has over 3 million and Marcus Butler has 2.6 million. Every time they have a new video, they can spread the word to millions of people. How many followers can you influence? To use your social networks effectively to promote your vlog, you must first grow your number of followers. If you can do that organically through interacting with people, posting interesting content and collaborating with the right people – in essence, if you develop a clever social media strategy – people will be more likely to click on your YouTube links when you post them.

The word 'strategy' is key. Popularity on social media is not a matter of luck. People don't follow you because of posts about what you eat for breakfast (unless you're a cookery vlogger), and they don't follow you to hear you moan about late public transport or poor customer service. They follow you because you're giving them something of value, which they find interesting, funny or useful. The moment you start to spam their feed by posting too many links to videos or by talking about irrelevant subjects is the moment your followers click *Unfollow*.

This chapter breaks down separate strategies to increase your influence on Facebook, Instagram, Twitter, Snapchat, Vine, YouNow and Pinterest, and each has a two-part approach. First, we'll look at simple tips that can help you increase your number of followers and likes. Then we'll look at ways of using each social network to engage followers so they remain with you for years, meaning they're more influenced by what you post and therefore more likely to watch your videos when you post them.

FACEBOOK
HOW TO INCREASE YOUR FACEBOOK 'LIKES'

With over a billion of the world's population on Facebook, it is vital to play the Facebook game correctly. If you get it right, you can find out what people like and potentially appeal to a lot of new viewers. If you added up the amount of time people spend on Facebook around the world, it could be as much as 700 billion hours a month – what great exposure! Moreover, by putting your time and energy into Facebook, you are reaching a market of people who actively use the Internet. As they're online already, it won't be difficult for them to click through to YouTube to view your vlog. The best form of marketing and brand exposure reaches people where they are.

To use Facebook effectively, you have to remember you are only as powerful as the number of people who 'like' you. Only the people who like you receive your news and updates. Therefore the goal of any vlogger is to increase their number of Facebook fan-page likes. To do this you should:

Name your page something interesting: Often, the name of the page will determine whether users click on it. If the name is boring, it is unlikely that users will bother reading the page. Once you reach a hundred likes, you cannot change the title of your page, so you need to get it right in the first place. The easiest thing to do is pick a name related to your vlog so that people can easily find the page.

Run competitions: By creating a contest that must involve Facebook interaction, you will increase likes in a short space of time. Clearly state in the rules that people have to like the page in order to enter the competition. If the prize is good, people will tell their friends about the competition and their friends will enter it too, further increasing your fan base.

Mention Facebook in your videos and in the YouTube description box: At the end of each of your YouTube videos, mention your Facebook fan page, and link to it within the first two lines of your description so that the link is always visible. A call to action giving people a reason to like you, such as access to extra content, can be extremely powerful. You could say: 'If you've enjoyed what you've seen so far, like us on Facebook for regular updates and cool behind-the-scenes photos!'

Update Facebook regularly: Although this seems obvious, many vloggers fall at this hurdle. Some only update Facebook when they have a new vlog to promote. You should aim to update Facebook at least once a day, especially because updating Facebook is a lot easier than making and editing a video. Give people a reason to keep checking in with you.

Pay Facebook to advertise your page: This is possibly one of the quickest ways to gain followers. Visit Facebook.com/advertising to create your campaign. You will have to surrender sensitive information about you and your brand, but this means your ads will only appear on Facebook accounts of people who fit your targeted demographic. You can set the ad budget, but remember that you get results based on how much you spend.

Join pages that relate to yours: This sounds obvious, but it really does work. If you like pages similar to yours and start up conversations on them, you will instantly get noticed. You could even post content from your site to these pages if it is relevant to the conversation within the community. This will not only gain you more likes, but will put your content out there. It is possible the owner of the page may take the content down, but if you create enough buzz around it then it is more difficult for it to be removed. It may be an advantage to you if the post is removed, as the fans of that page will be interested in the rest of the story – which could give you automatic Facebook likes.

Link to other social networking sites: Curiosity will naturally send your Twitter, Instagram and Pinterest followers to your Facebook page. Whenever you add information about yourself to a user or contributor page, make sure you include your Facebook link too.

Promote your page everywhere: Never miss an opportunity to promote your page. Whenever you make a video, always reference your Facebook page. Don't overkill it, but one link per video is acceptable, combined with an appropriate card or annotation. If you are collaborating with another vlogger, ask the other vlogger to ensure your social media links are in the description box. Tell anyone you meet about it and, if you have business cards, get your Facebook page link printed on it. Adding a link to your email signature line is also effective.

USING FACEBOOK TO PROMOTE YOUR VLOG

It's vital to consistently post things that engage and interest your readers, or they'll think you're spamming them and unlike your page. So what kind of content should you be putting up? Have a look at your favourite vloggers' Facebook pages for inspiration.

You should see that the content on their Facebook pages is very varied. They don't just post links to their videos and say 'Watch this!' There might be teasers for upcoming YouTube videos to get people excited for what's to come. There could be behind-the-scenes shots and outtakes, showing that the vloggers can laugh at themselves. Some vloggers may involve their audiences by setting up a Facebook poll to determine what their fans want to see next. Others post interesting links to news stories about what's happening in their niche. For example, beauty vloggers may mention new product releases, and fashion vloggers may talk about a well-dressed celebrity and ask for their fans' opinions. A lot of vloggers have blogs related to their YouTube channels, and they share their blog posts and articles on their Facebook page.

Notice that all of the established vloggers update their Facebook page regularly. The more you entertain people with the content that you post to Facebook, the more inclined people will be to watch your videos when you post links to them.

Don't just post things and walk away. You wouldn't shout things to a friend and walk away before they'd had a chance to reply, would you? If you did this, then you wouldn't have many friends. The way to keep friends in real life is to interact with them. You listen to their responses and then you respond to their comments. You should be doing the same thing on Facebook, and monitoring the comments underneath the posts. With the rise of mobile devices, there's no excuse for posting something on Facebook and then disappearing for the rest of the day. You can monitor your Facebook activity while you're on the bus or queuing up in a shop. The more you reply to people, the more approachable and friendly you'll appear to your Facebook fans. People need to be treated like friends if you're to stand a chance of persuading them to do something like watching one of your vlogs.

Once you're posting and commenting regularly, you can share links to your vlogs and people will be more likely to click them. However, timing is important. Using your YouTube Analytics data, work out what time of day your videos get most views. This is the time you should be posting to Facebook as this is the time your audience is most active online. Also, are some of your audience located in different time zones geographically? If so, make sure you post at times international audiences are likely to be awake as well as times convenient to viewers in your country.

INSTAGRAM
HOW TO INCREASE YOUR INSTAGRAM FOLLOWERS

Instagram is the fastest-growing social network. More than 70 million photos are shared each day, making over 30 billion in total. However, the most interesting statistic, and the biggest reason to cultivate a loyal network of Instagram followers, is the fact there are now more Instagram users than Twitter users. As of September 2015, there were 320 million monthly active Twitter users, according to the About section on Twitter's company website. In the same month, Instagram reported 400 million monthly active users on its press page, which was a growth of 100 million in just nine months.

An advantage of social networks getting larger is that potentially you can reach more people and tell them about your vlog. Conversely, one disadvantage is that it's harder to get noticed in a never-ending stream of Instagram posts made by millions of others around the world.

If you want to stand out, achieve more Instagram followers and get more likes for your photos and videos, this is what you need to do:

Use hashtags: As you may know from experiences with Twitter, hashtags allow users to search for subjects that interest them. If you caption your photos and videos with hashtags, you'll come up in search results.

Using just a few hashtags in the captions of your images could get them noticed by people who don't already follow you, and who may not have any connections with you other than their interest in those hashtags. In essence, hashtags help you reach more people.

Use trending hashtags: While it's possible to make anything you want into a hashtag – the name of your vlog, a short saying or random words linked together – you'll get more exposure if you use popular hashtags that people are likely to be searching for.

There are two ways to find out what's trending on Instagram and which hashtags will get you more likes. The first is the website Top Hashtags (top-hashtags.com/instagram), which is updated every ten seconds so you can see what's trending at the exact moment you're posting. The other tool is the app Tags 4 Likes, which can be downloaded from the app store of any smartphone. Scroll through the app to find the subject that your Instagram post is about and it will bring up a list of relevant hashtags that you can copy into your post.

Make use of the first hundred characters: Your followers see only the first hundred characters of your Instagram description, so if it's longer than that, your followers will have to click on the image to read the whole description. Therefore you need to summarise what your image or video is about in the first few words. Try to be attention-grabbing with a witty or funny caption, as that's more likely to make people want to read on. Use the majority of your hashtags after the hundred-character limit, so the first part of your description is seen to be interesting rather than hashtag overload.

Comment on other people's Instagram posts: Search for the hashtags you've entered into your description to find people with similar interests. When you see that someone's posted a really cool photo relevant to what you've posted about, like it and tell them how great it is. The more you do this, the more likely people are to check you out in return, and if they like your posts they'll follow you. Always comment on the Instagram pics of vloggers who inspire you or are influential in your field. Even if they don't notice you, you could make friends with some of the other people who are commenting underneath that vlogger's post. You already have one thing in common – you both follow that vlogger – and if you add something interesting to the conversation, the other commenter is more likely to check out your Instagram account and follow you. It might not happen straight away, but the more you comment, the more you will recognise other users and slowly gain credibility.

Share the best bits: All the hashtags in the world can't compensate for a boring photo or video. Instagram is a visual platform, so the image or video you share needs to grab people's attention. Fortunately, YouTube is also a visual platform, so if you've created a high-quality video with lots of fun content you'll have plenty to choose from when you're thinking about what to post on Instagram.

You could share previews, short video clips, outtakes or behind-the-scenes pictures and videos. If you're collaborating with another vlogger, take a selfie with them and post it on Instagram to promote your upcoming collaboration video. If you're a beauty vlogger, give sneak peeks at the stunning results of the tutorial you'll be posting in the next few days. If you're a prankster or comedy vlogger, post a picture of someone's reaction. You could even post the YouTube thumbnail you've chosen for your next video to build a buzz before it goes online.

Share bright photos: Research proves well-lit images are more liked than dark ones. Dan Zarella is a social media scientist who worked at Hubspot, and went on to write four books about the science of social media. He also writes regular posts about social media on his blog (danzarella.com). Dan conducted an experiment in the hope of finding out what makes some images more popular than others. He picked 1 million Instagram users and analysed a total of 1.5 million photos from across their accounts. One significant result was that bright and colourful photos had 592 per cent more likes than dark photos – that's a huge difference!

Include faces: Dan Zarella used face-detection analysis to find out that photos with one or more human faces in them received more likes than those without faces. There was a 35 per cent difference between the two, which means a lot when you're starting out and trying to grow an audience.

Tag people: If you've mentioned a brand or person in your YouTube video, then tag them in any Instagram posts related to that video. When someone is tagged, they'll see a notification in their feed. If they like the image, they might repost it and this means you'll gain exposure among their network of followers.

Stay relevant: You've worked hard to create a brand image for your vlog. Don't ruin that by posting pictures that aren't 'on-message'. Write down a few words that sum up your brand, and always pick images from your videos and daily life that reflect those words. Don't suddenly post scenes from a horror movie if you have a beauty blog – it will really confuse people. You'll get more likes if you have a reputation for being consistent.

Post at key times: There's no point in posting when your followers are sleeping. Use your YouTube Analytics to see when your audience is most active, and post during those times. Be aware of global time differences. If some of your viewers are in America, do one post a day at a convenient time for them and another at a convenient time for those in the UK. However, remember what counts is quality not quantity – don't feel under pressure to post if you can't find a great image, as dark and dull pictures give off the impression that you're a dull person.

Use your Facebook network: As Instagram owns Facebook, it's easy to find Facebook friends who are using Instagram. Once you follow them, they should follow you back, seeing as you already like each other on one social network.

Find your friends by navigating to your profile page. At the top right of the screen you'll see a wheel icon that indicates

Settings. Click on the wheel, and select *Find friends >Find friends on Facebook.*

Use your email signature and business cards: Every time you send an email it's an opportunity to tell someone about your Instagram account, so make sure there's a link in your email sign-off and that the link is clickable and directs people to your Instagram page.

Business cards contain all the information someone needs to contact you, and your Instagram account should be included in that. As so many people use Instagram, chances are that the person who's receiving the card has an Instagram account too.

HOW TO USE INSTAGRAM TO PROMOTE YOUR VLOG

A mistake many newbies make is that they don't properly utilise their Instagram bio. The bio section is designed to briefly explain what you do and your motivation for doing it, and to contain a link to refer people to where you want them to go – i.e. to your latest video or your YouTube channel.

Every time you post something related to a specific video, the description of that post should say: 'Want more? Check out the link to my YouTube channel [or latest video] in my bio!' That way people will have to navigate to your Instagram homepage to see your bio, and when they're there they'll see more of your photos and videos as well as the link to check you out on YouTube.

To keep your audience engaged, you need to give users exclusive material that they won't see in your videos. Otherwise there's no motivation for people to follow you on Instagram if everything you post is duplicated on your YouTube channel. Make it seem as if Instagram users get extra access into your life through following you. Take a behind-the-scenes tour. Give an extra beauty tip that really completes or complements your last tutorial. Share secrets and tips. Feature a funny moment in your day and let people into your daily life.

Instagram is about being personal, so make sure your followers can see your personality in what you post. If you post quality, exclusive content, your Instagram followers will not only like and comment on your Instagram posts, they'll also be more interested in checking out your full videos on YouTube.

Interaction on Instagram is just as important as it is on Facebook. These are social networks, and being sociable requires interaction rather than broadcasting what you're up to and walking away. You could post a shot from your most recent YouTube video and ask for feedback. You could also make an image and overlay text on it to ask a question of your audience, or you could ask for their opinions in your image's caption. However you decide to start a conversation with your audience, be sure to interact with them in the comments. Direct your replies to them by mentioning their usernames; for example, you could say '@Instagram User, Thanks for the feedback! What topic would you like me to cover in an upcoming video?'

To be really successful on Instagram and engage users, the trick is to be yourself. It sounds simple, but you need to show off what makes you unique, rather than worrying about what more popular users have done to get likes. When you're genuine, you're more likely to be liked and followed, and once you've won people over with your Instagram personality they'll want to click on the link in your bio to watch your vlogs.

CASE STUDY: POPPY DELEVINGNE

Model Poppy Delevingne has more than 1 million followers on Instagram. Being able to post photos with her famous friends and relatives like Alexa Chung and Cara Delevingne has helped to grow her profile, and her followers have stuck around because she consistently posts beautiful images.

In an interview with *Marie Claire* magazine, Poppy shared her top Instagram tricks:

Pick the background: 'If you're wearing a great outfit, taking a photo in front of an office door or messy bedroom simply won't do it justice. If I do an Outfit of the Day, for me it's all about the background. For example, a great palm or a peachy-pink wall that complements the outfit you're wearing.'

Take lots of pictures: 'Great Instagrams always come with a little help from your friends (or any willing human). My poor husband has to stand there and I say, "Take ten!" If you take one, that's not going to be the perfect shot. So take ten at least!'

Make a face: 'I'm really bad at selfies. So I've decided, being so bad at them, that I just do a really good frog-face. When you feel like a straight-up smile or serious face looks too awkward or posed, opt for a funnier one.'

Have fun: This one is a bit obvious, but if you have to force it, leave it. The more fun you're having in a selfie, the better it is.'

TWITTER

Twitter is not used by as many people as Facebook, but it's a more powerful tool for vloggers due to the intelligence of information you can gain from the Twitter software. You can use a programme like TweetReach (tweetreach.com) to learn how many people you've reached from just one tweet. You could use this information and compare it with your YouTube Analytics to see how many of your Twitter followers proceed to engage with the video. Through TweetReach you can also keep track of what subjects your followers find interesting. If they keep choosing to retweet your messages about a particular make-up brand, then you know that brand is popular and you should be covering it more in your vlogs.

People have written entire books about how to use Twitter for personal use, how to use it for business and even personal stories about how Twitter has changed their lives. I do recommend purchasing at least one of these to get more information, but I have summed up the basics below.

HOW TO INCREASE TWITTER FOLLOWERS

Consider the following strategies:

Tweet at peak times: Monitor when people are tweeting the most and start doing the same. Although there is always a steady influx of tweets, studies have shown that top Twitter activity usually takes place between 10am and 4pm, with most responses being tweeted between 1pm and 2pm. There is little or no point tweeting during the middle of the night, unless you are aiming your tweets to people in different time zones.

Interact: You will never get your follower numbers up if you don't interact. Twitter is an online community, and with that you have to be social. Although it is important to tweet, if you do it too often you are likely to lose followers. Stick to one topic at a time and follow it through. Wait a fair amount of time before changing topic or retweeting someone else's message, to avoid overkill. And if anyone does engage and ask you questions, make sure you answer him or her.

Target popular and influential Twitter users: Following, tweeting and retweeting people who are well-respected in your niche will create a buzz around your account. You may not get these influential users following you, but other people will pick up on you and follow.

Whatever industry you're in, you'll find there are people tweeting about it who have more followers than you. If you're a fashion vlogger you may target a designer, if you cover beauty you may target a make-up artist and if you talk about tech you may target a high-profile gadget vlogger. Use the Twitter search box to find those tweeting about similar subjects, see who has the most followers and ask them something interesting to grab their attention.

It's important to plan what you're going to write, as you want your tweet to stand out from the hundreds of others that popular person receives daily. Motivational quotes, funny scenarios or thought-provoking questions are the best. If at first you don't succeed, try, try again. By monitoring what that person has been saying to other people and referencing it, you can make it seem as if you have a genuine interest in what they have to say. They'll notice you in the end.

Make people aware of your Twitter page: Make sure the link to your Twitter profile is in the first few lines of every YouTube description box and talk about it in your videos. Also, connect your Twitter to your Facebook, Instagram and Pinterest profiles.

Utilise Twitter hashtags: This little Twitter tool is vital in getting your tweets out there. Lots of people search Twitter for information about the subject they're interested in, so if you hashtag the topic you are talking about, it will make it a lot easier for people to see your tweets. For example, if you were tweeting about the Olympics in 2016, you would use the hashtag #Olympics2016. When other Twitter users search for tweets on this subject, your content will come up in their results.

Once others see you're both interested in the same topic, they may start to follow you for more updates. Conversely, if you notice others tweeting about similar things, then you could follow them. People receive a notification each time they get a new follower, so they might check out your recent tweets, notice that you share an interest and start to follow you back. For example, if you're doing a vlog mentioning Beyoncé, you should search Twitter and look at all the recent tweets from anyone who has used #Beyoncé. If someone has posted a lot of tweets and used the hashtag Beyoncé each time, you can deduce that they are a Beyoncé expert and start to follow them. Hopefully, once they see you're following them, they'll click on your Twitter profile, see you're also a Beyoncé fan and follow you back as you have similar interests.

However, watch out for hashtag overload. Stuffing your tweets with hashtags is confusing and blinds viewers to what you're actually saying. It's best to use one well-picked hashtag than to make every word a hashtag.

Tweet photos: People love looking at what someone is doing as well as reading a status update. Get a reputation for giving your followers a little bit more than they'd get in an average Twitter message, and they're guaranteed to tell their friends about you. This works especially well if you give people access into somewhere they could never normally hope to be, such as backstage when you're filming or any cool events you get invited to because of your vlog.

Mention brands: Whenever you mention or review a brand in your YouTube video, you can use Twitter to draw the brand's attention to it. Your mention is great exposure for the brand and in return they should retweet your tweet, favourite it or share your video. When they do this, your tweet instantly gets exposure to their audience, which will tend to be both large and made up of people who could be interested in your vlogs.

Stay current: Twitter moves very fast, so be careful not to be left behind. Keeping up with newsworthy events is important as people want to talk about the here and now, not what happened two weeks ago. They want to know what is going on at that particular moment. Being a few hours late to a conversation can be detrimental, as it limits your exposure to a new audience.

Start a contest: Just like with Facebook, hosting a Twitter competition will increase your followers fast. Get people to answer questions or retweet the competition tweet and you'll be seen by all their followers. Some of those followers may decide to follow you. Make sure you hashtag the competition when you announce it, as this will enable more users to see it in search results. The more people who see it, the more they can spread the word.

USING TWITTER TO PROMOTE YOUR VLOG

Twitter etiquette is similar to Facebook etiquette in the sense that posting multiple links to your videos, or reposting information telling people to look at your videos, is considered spamming. Nobody wants to see the same content over and over again in their Twitter timeline, and people will quickly unfollow those who are cluttering up the timeline with what they perceive to be junk.

If you want people to take you seriously and follow the links to your videos when you post them, you need to tweet multiple times a day about interesting subjects, giving your followers information that entertains or educates them. With Facebook, you can get away with posting once a day, but Twitter moves so fast that if you only posted one tweet a day it would get lost in the Twitter mix. This doesn't need to mean that you're tweeting all day and night. Use TweetReach and your YouTube Analytics to see what times your audience is most active online. This is when you should be on Twitter to chat with your audience and show them how cool you can be 24/7 – not just in that three-minute vlog you post every week.

Things you can post to mix up the content of your tweets include links to news happening in your niche, your thoughts on this news, inspirational quotes, attention-grabbing or funny photos and updates of interesting things that have happened during your day.

To really grab people's attention you could make a funny animated gif based on a video and share it on Twitter. The right gif has the potential to go viral, thus dramatically increasing your exposure. Animated gifs are several images presented in sequence to create the illusion of animation, which is often grainy or jerky but that's part of the fun. gifs of celebrities pulling funny faces, frames of movie scenes or animals' odd behaviour are often shared around the world to millions of people.

You can create a gif online by just adding 'gif' after the www in the URL of your YouTube video, for example www.gifyoutube. com/myvideo. Once you type that in, you'll be taken to a simple gif-making page that lets you cut out a section of the video and export it. Select the point at which you want to start the gif, then how long you want it to be, and you're done. Remember that the most popular gifs capture the most unique or attention-grabbing moments of a video, so it's worth paying close attention to make sure you pick the right part.

Question your Twitter followers regularly. For example, you could ask your followers what they'd like to see in your next YouTube video, or if they had a good or bad experience with a particular product and would like to tell you about it. Ask them about their thoughts on a topic you're vlogging about, or what their favourite tips and tricks are for dealing with a relevant situation.

Once you've asked the question, make sure to read the responses and respond to them too. Stay in the conversation and keep it going. As more people see the conversations taking place on their Twitter feeds, they'll start joining in and sharing their thoughts, helping to create more awareness for your channel.

Reward everyone who has taken the time to mention you in a tweet by responding. This shows your followers you care about and appreciate them. When they mention you in a tweet, respond or retweet their tweet. When they tweet to share one of your YouTube videos, you can thank them.

Twitter is a more effective platform than Facebook for connecting you with your YouTube viewers and making them feel like you care about them, because you can respond to people individually rather than commenting on a group post. People watch your videos because they want to be your friend, and if you keep responding to them on Twitter, they'll feel like the friendship means something and will watch more videos out of loyalty.

What else do friends have in common? Sometimes they party together. You could host your own virtual party, or group Twitter chat, in the hope that everyone who's interested in the same subjects as you joins in. Twitter chats are great for audience engagement and it will help with vlog traffic if you aim to host one every month at least.

To start your Twitter chat, announce in advance that you're going to be hosting a chat for a specific amount of time on a particular day. Tell users that they can participate by using your custom hashtag in their tweets during the chat (e.g. #YouTubeChannelNameChat). All tweets with the chat's hashtag will be grouped together, and you can carry on a great conversation with your audience about topics relevant to them. Twitter chats can also help exposure, as people who follow your chat participants on Twitter will learn about your YouTube channel on their newsfeed, expanding your reach even more.

It's advisable to prepare questions in advance of your Twitter chat. People are often shy to get started and nobody likes to be the first to respond, so you need to have a back-up plan. Tweet some questions ahead of the chat so that people can prepare and feel more confident about their answers. Or ask some of your friends to join in the chat at the start; once your viewers see that you're popular, they'll want to join your conversation.

After your chat is done, keep interacting with the people who took part. Start by posting a tweet to thank everyone who contributed. Next, create a YouTube video about the Twitter chat, giving mentions to the participants. Talk about the key topics and say how people reacted to certain subjects. Thank everyone for taking part and invite them to join in future chats – you may even want to set a date now so that people can make sure they're free for the next one.

VINE
HOW TO GROW YOUR VINE FOLLOWERS

Vine is Twitter's social platform for six-second looping video, which can be viewed with the Vine app or shared on Twitter or Facebook. It launched in January 2013, and according to the company over 200 million people are watching Vine videos every month as of January 2016. While it's not as fast-growing as Instagram, the fact that it's a social media platform dedicated to video means that vloggers wanting to promote their work and reach more people need to have a presence on it. To get started on Vine, you should:

Update your profile: When you sign up for the Vine app, you need to enter your email address or your Twitter account details. If you choose the Twitter option, your Vine profile is automatically imported from Twitter. However, it's a good idea to adapt your profile for Vine by mentioning the type of videos you'll be uploading – fashion, beauty, gaming, comedy etc. This is important because one way people discover others to follow is through the People Search function, which lets people search for others who upload videos about categories they're interested in. If your Vine profile doesn't mention what you do, then you'll be invisible to your ideal Vine audience as you won't come up in search results.

Connect Twitter and Facebook: This will enable you to share videos on these platforms and alert your Twitter and Facebook followers that you have a Vine account. It's a great way to get some followers at the start. To connect your accounts from the main Vine menu, go to *Profile > Settings* and then scroll down until you reach the Social Networks section. Since Vine is a Twitter product, Vine allows you to search for Twitter contacts that you'd like to connect with on Vine. Once you add them, it's highly likely they'll follow you back if they already follow you on Twitter. To do this, first connect Twitter, then go to *Profile >Settings*. Scroll down and you'll see the Friends section, where you can click the *Find People* option.

Use popular hashtags: Users of Vine can use the Explore menu to find videos about subjects they're interested in. The subjects are organised into groups via hashtags, such as #howto, #food or #pets. You should visit the Explore menu and take note of what hashtags there are and include some of those hashtags when you upload your video. Don't be afraid to add tags that aren't on the Explore menu as well, because people can search by tag from within the app – they're not always using the Explore menu. Use several tags to improve your chances of being found.

Comment and interact: As with any other social network, it is very important to participate and socialise with other users in order to get noticed.

Start by using the Search feature to enter tags relating to your interests. This will allow you to find people who consistently post the types of videos you enjoy and who cover similar subjects to you. Now follow them. If you are interesting to them, they will often follow you right back. Make sure you've posted a video or two and filled out your profile completely for this to be as effective as possible. Nobody will follow you back if you lack content.

Like and comment on all the videos that you enjoy, because when you like or comment on a post it will automatically be shown in the Activity feed of all the other people who have commented or liked the post. This tactic can attract a lot of new followers quickly if you apply it properly. Avoid being spammy, but be smart about your likes and comments – there is nothing wrong with ensuring you always comment on posts you enjoyed which have a lot of comments or likes already.

HOW TO USE VINE TO PROMOTE YOUR VLOGS

A six-second video loop is very different to a three- to five-minute vlog, and a mistake many vloggers make is that they pick a random six seconds from their vlog and post it to Vine, hoping for the best. To be successful on Vine you need to understand the medium, and this means doing some research. You should spend time researching what works well on Vine and then do something similar, adapting it slightly to fit the image of your vlog and brand.

To get a feel of what works well on Vine, you should regularly browse the Editor's Picks and Popular sections within the Vine app. You can access these under Explore on the main menu. Also, the Search by Tag feature at the top of the Explore menu is invaluable, as it allows you to see what Vines are being posted by others in your niche.

Make sure you post a variety of videos. While it's good to post previews of the best bits of your videos, you need to give people more than what they can find on your YouTube channel. Give your Vine followers a sneak peek into your behind-the-scenes activities, maybe showing the process of editing a video, preparing the set or picking what you're going to wear. Or you could highlight fun bloopers and outtakes, showing times you fell over or made a mess. The more insight you give into your real life the better, and humour always goes down well.

As soon as you've posted a Vine video, make contact with people who are interested in the same things as you to get them to notice it. Rather than sitting back and hoping people will find your hashtags, go out and find people who share your passions and make them aware of your presence. To do this, every time you upload a video on a specific topic such as make-up or eyeliner, explore the related tags on Vine that other users have posted, like #makeup, #eyeliner, #beauty, #howto, #beautytutorial etc. Like and comment on those videos and follow any you really like. The more comments and likes you make, the more people will follow you back. Once they follow you and notice you're consistently posting interesting or amusing Vines about their favourite subjects, they'll want to see more of your videos on YouTube.

SNAPCHAT
HOW TO INCREASE YOUR SNAPCHAT FOLLOWERS
Snapchat is a fun messaging app. You can take a photo or a video, then add a caption, doodle or lens graphic over the top, and send it to a friend. Friends will be able to view it for ten seconds before it expires. Alternatively, you can add moments to your Story, which is a twenty-four-hour collection of your photos and videos that you can choose to broadcast to the world or just to your followers. Snapchat's Story function is the reason vloggers can do well out of Snapchat. You're experienced in making videos about your life, and you can show that off on Snapchat. What's even better is that there's no need to spend hours editing. You film the fun parts of the day, and Snapchat automatically makes the Story.

The growth of Snapchat's mobile video traffic is staggering. It started off in 2011 as a hit with teens and young adults who wanted to share silly things visible for short periods of time without lasting incriminating evidence. When companies and celebrities realised its popularity, they got on board, and now most celebrities have Snapchat accounts. This has widened the demographic of Snapchat, as older fans of celebrities started using the app to get exclusive content from their idols. Vloggers need to be on Snapchat, whatever the age of viewer they're aiming at, because Snapchat's demographic is constantly growing.

Vlogger Casey Neistat recently published a video stating that

Snapchat would kill Facebook. He argued that the younger generation currently use Snapchat more than Facebook, therefore new generations would prefer to join Snapchat, leaving Facebook with ageing account-holders. Business statistics do seem to back up Neistat's theory. *Fortune* magazine published a report in January 2016 explaining that Snapchat is catching up with Facebook in terms of video views. In aggregate, Snapchat users viewed more than 7 billion videos per day as of January 2016. Another report by the *Financial Times* found that, between June and November 2015, Snapchat's traffic more than tripled to 6 billion per day. That's a staggering rate of growth! In comparison, Facebook last reported that its users watched 8 billion videos per day on both desktop and mobile at the end of December 2015. It took Facebook eleven years to achieve that eight billion, with steady growth from its inception in 2004 until the current date. Snapchat has achieved 7 billion in just five years. It's little wonder, therefore, that Facebook reportedly offered to buy Snapchat for $3 billion, and that Snapchat founder Evan Spiegel turned them down because he was so confident in the growth potential of his platform.

As each Snapchat story lasts only twenty-four hours, there's a sense of urgency and compulsion to watch stories before they expire. If somebody's favourite celebrity has made a story and viewers know they have just twenty-four hours to watch it, they'll check back constantly to see if there's anything new. While checking, they may spot a story from a friend, which they feel compelled to watch before it expires. Nobody likes to feel like they've missed out, so people check Snapchat several times a day to make sure they're up to date with the latest news and gossip happening in their friendship circles. *Business Insider* magazine recently did a survey that found the average Snapchat user checked their account fifteen times a day! Vloggers who upload daily content to Snapchat can make use of this sense of urgency and use it to create a fan base who crave their stories. Once the fans are hooked on a vlogger's stories, they'll head to that vlogger's YouTube channel to see more of their work.

When you download Snapchat for the first time, you'll see it's not your typical social media site as it doesn't allow you to find or discover people or brands. So how are people going to discover you? To stand out on Snapchat you should:

Use Snapcodes: Every Snapchat user is given a Snapcode, which is Snapchat's version of a QR code. To add a friend on Snapchat, users simply open the camera within the Snapchat app and focus it on a friend's Snapcode. Therefore to get noticed by people, you need to share your Snapcode with them. Snapchat allows you to download a vector version of your Snapcode, which you put can put on websites or blogs, posters, business cards or even stickers. Make it easy for people to add you!

Tell your Facebook friends: Take a screenshot of your Snapcode and upload it to Facebook, inviting your online friends to follow you on Snapchat by holding their phones over the screen. This is a great way to transfer your existing Facebook friends over to Snapchat.

Tease your Instagram followers: Post an intriguing Instagram picture that hints you're up to something exciting, and then write in the caption that your followers need to head to Snapchat to see more. Perhaps you're going overseas, or to a fun event. Either way, post an attention-grabbing photo and say you'll be making a Snapchat story about it which will contain all the backstage goss.

Create content from day one: You can't be discovered if you don't have any content, so make stories and take snaps even if you have no followers. Then send your best snaps to the people you follow, as this is possible even if they are not following you back. Sharing a well-thought-out photo or attention-grabbing video is a great way to get discovered and gain followers.

Spy on popular Snapchatters: Look at what other vloggers in your niche are doing and make a note of what's worked well for them. They are doing something right to build a following, so pay attention as they create and share their content. Then try a similar technique, but add your own spin to it.

You'll find that the most popular Snapchatters are using the app to give a thorough insight into their daily life. Each individual video they create reflects something that's happened to them and their take on it. When they've pieced together all these insights and made a story, viewers are left wishing they lived like that Snapchatter. Popular Snapchatters can find humour in the most mundane of situations. Spend a bit of time on Snapchat and you'll find the most popular Snapchatters have the creative ability to build a dramatic narrative out of anything, from shopping in a grocery store to cooking pancakes.

Be creative: The best Snapchatters add entertaining text and emojis to their snaps and videos. Taking a cool picture or video is only half the battle. The other half is to present your take on what's captured in the picture or video in a creative and witty way.

Add text to the picture by tapping on the image until a text box appears. You can alter the size of the text and change the colour in various ways. Look for the big T icon at the top as this indicates the Text function. Tap on it and it will make the text large and left-aligned. Tap again, and it will centre. Select the text when large, and you can use the colour palette on the side to change colours. Use two fingers to pinch the text smaller or stretch it larger, plus rotate it however you like.

You can also draw on your image by using the pencil icon in the top-right corner. You can change colours multiple times, just by lifting your finger then selecting a new colour.

Filters enable you to add the time, temperature, speed while travelling in a vehicle and your location details. Once you've created a snap, swipe your finger left or right on the snap draft to preview all the available filters. If you can't see them, go back to your Snapchat settings and make sure the Filters toggle is enabled.

Reach out to other Snapchatters: Watch other Stories to find opportunities to contribute. Influencers love creating content that gets their followers engaged and involved in their story. Participate in influencers' Stories by sending them creative snaps. They might just feature one in their Story. Doing this and getting featured exposes you to the other Snapchatter's audience.

Approach other Snapchatters and ask if they want to collaborate with you for a day so you could make a Story featuring each other. Don't be afraid to reach out and ask. It's okay if you get a 'no'; it just means 'not right now'. Keep making more great content and approach them again at a later date. You'll be surprised by how quickly others say yes to you when you have more followers.

HOW TO USE SNAPCHAT TO PROMOTE YOUR VLOGS

Snapchat users feel like they're friends with the Snapchatters they follow. They like to be informed of what's happening in that Snapchatter's life, just as you like to know what's happening with people in your friendship groups. But what don't they like? They don't like to be ignored, just like you would stop being friends with someone in real life if they weren't making any effort. Therefore, the way to keep people following you is to make sure they continue to feel valued. Always follow-back people who follow you. Try to answer back every individual message sent to you. This might be tough to do once you start gaining more followers, but try your best to get to as many people as you can. Engagement is key to building loyal followers.

Keep people interested by hosting competitions exclusively on Snapchat, so that the only way people know about the competition is by following you on Snapchat. Keep the prize and the entry criteria relevant to your videos: so if you're a beauty vlogger, the prize could be a goody-bag containing all the make-up you used in a particular video. Entrance criteria could be people sending you snaps of how they followed your tutorial and copied it. As entries come in, take screenshots and post all the appropriate entries to your Stories feed for the world to see before announcing a winner.

To make your Stories stand out from the other Stories a Snapchat user has in their feed, you need to actively encourage them to check out yours. To do this, create a photo summing up one of the coolest bits of your Story and caption it with a call to action like 'View my Story now,' or 'View my Story before it expires in three hours.' Setting a deadline creates more urgency.

Another trick to rank higher in your friends' newsfeeds is by constantly updating your Story. Snapchat displays Stories based on when the snap was last updated, so as your viewer scrolls through their feed, they will see the last updated snap from their friends first. Adding to your Story throughout the day and night helps to move and keep your Story at the top of your followers' Stories feed. The best way to gain additions to your Story is to ask your viewers to share or contribute to the current Story. Get them to engage by asking questions like 'What did you think?' or 'Snap me your reactions!' You can then take a picture of their picture and add them to your Story. This will also make your Snapchat users feel valued, and when followers feel like you care, they're more likely to stay loyal.

Sharing behind-the-scenes content is a great way to get your Snapchat users excited about upcoming videos. Creating a Story based on exclusive content from an upcoming video and the making-of process will make them excited about watching the full episode when it's uploaded to YouTube. Make sure to keep the quality high and attention-grabbing, because you're competing with other vloggers for that Snapchat user's attention.

CASE STUDY: POPPY JAMIE

Poppy Jamie hosts the talk show *Pillow Talk* on Snapchat's Discover Channel, which is watched by 100 million Snapchat users. She's also hired by brands to take over their Snapchat accounts during key events; she managed the Lancôme

Snapchat account at the 2016 BAFTA Awards and the River Island account during Glastonbury 2015.

Poppy recently gave an interview to the beauty website *Byrdie*, sharing her top Snapchat tips. This is what she said:

Be honest: 'This is so important! It's fine to Snapchat with no make-up on and allow the user to see you naturally. Actually the more honest you are the better your feed. I love watching the transformation from no make-up to full glam look!'

Don't hold back: 'Post as much as you want. You're not clogging up newsfeeds, your snaps are just added to your own individual story.'

Be funny: 'Don't take yourself too seriously. Each snap is deleted after twenty-four hours, so there is no need to worry about being silly and having fun with it. On Snapchat no one can see how many likes each snap has, so all social pressure is removed. Embrace this!'

Get animated: 'I love how you can now play with different animations, if you press down the screen while looking at your face. Usually there's about seven to choose from, and it's hilarious seeing your face distorted, adorned with hearts and kisses or transformed into a cat.'

Tell a story: 'Rather than just snapping a finished make-up look or haircut like you would for Instagram, Snapchat is the platform to show the process. Users feel like they are getting the inside track – my fans especially love seeing make-up tips.'

Mix it up: 'It's great to get creative with a mix of videos and pictures. With videos there are fast-forward and slow-mo effects which can be really effective and engaging.'

Be original: Post all the cool and weird things you see. Snapchat is all about sharing your eyes and ears with your followers. Pick things that you find interesting and will send a positive message.

Snap steady: 'Hold your phone steady when videoing, otherwise you can make watchers feel sick with shuddering shots!'

YOUNOW

HOW TO INCREASE YOUR YOUNOW FOLLOWERS

YouNow is a live broadcasting app and desktop website. At any given moment, you can visit YouNow and tune in to people filming what they're up to at that exact moment. When Endemol's TV format *Big Brother* started, viewers could go to the Endemol website to see live streams from the house twenty-four hours a day. YouNow has a similar format, except the live broadcasts are coming from everyday filmmakers and there are thousands of live broadcasts to choose from, sorted into hashtags. There's everything from watching people playing music to watching people eat or sleep.

YouNow's 4 million members argue it's more addictive than Snapchat. While a Snapchat story is visible for twenty-four hours, YouNow is instantaneous. If you're not watching at that exact moment, then you're missing out.

Another appealing feature of YouNow is that video-makers can communicate directly with their fans, and devoted fans can pay money to get the video-makers' attention. As the video streams, there's a chatbox by the side of it. All viewers are welcome to leave comments in the chatbox or simply watch the chat that is developing. The most popular stars on YouNow have a special talent to watch the chatbox as they broadcast and then respond to as many questions or dares as possible. However, the more followers a YouNow star has, the more difficult it is for them to spot individual comments because they could be receiving hundreds each minute. If a viewer really wants to get their comment noticed, they can pay to have their comment featured at the top of the chatbox. This is done with points that the user purchases with real money from YouNow. The money is split between YouNow and the video-maker.

Success on YouNow is defined by how many people are watching your live broadcast. The more people who tune in and like you, the more you will be promoted on the site, as you will be at the top of the list of videos shown when viewers search by hashtag. It's great practice for vloggers because you can see the results immediately. When you're lively and you chat about fun things, people tune in and like you. Conversely, when your energy levels drop, people start to leave the broadcast.

YouNow followers tend to be super-loyal, especially the ones that pay to tip you, and so growing a following on YouNow could lead to a big increase in YouTube subscribers. Also, YouTube networks have started watching YouNow to discover the YouTube stars of the future in the same way a record label would send an A&R rep to scout bands at open mic nights. To stand out on YouNow, you could:

Use your other social networks: Make sure your YouNow link is in your Twitter, Instagram and Facebook bio. To add a YouNow icon to your YouTube channel, go to My Channel, and click the pencil icon in the top-right corner of your cover photo. Then choose *Edit links*. Type *YouNow* into the *Link title* section and paste your YouNow profile URL in the *URL* section.

Watch other broadcasters in your niche: Before broadcasting, spend a few weeks watching the most popular broadcasters in the category that you'll be joining. What are they doing well? Can you do something similar but add your own unique twist to it? Plan what you are going to do before you start broadcasting so you don't freeze up when you go live.

Poll the audience: Ask people 'yes or no' questions to get them engaged. Silly questions also work well, like: 'Type "1" in the chat if you want me to do a backflip, type "2" if you want me to eat a goldfish!'

Have something interesting to say: Those who beg for likes and wait for audience suggestions aren't as popular as the broadcasters who start off with something fun to say, and then alter their broadcast once their audience joins in. What kinds of things do you talk about in your vlogs? Talk about similar things in your broadcasts, but give them a more behind-the-scenes feel and pay attention to the comments. People will interrupt you and ask you to do weird things. You don't have to do them, but it will result in more likes and hence more popularity. It's more fun for an audience to throw someone off track than to suggest tasks to someone with a blank face and no ideas. Make the audience feel like they're being cheeky, not like they're doing all the work.

Smile: Broadcasters who look like they're having fun are more likely to keep the attention of their audience. People watch YouNow to be entertained, and if they can't get that from you they'll find someone who is livelier. You'll find it's great practice for keeping up your energy levels in your vlogs, because the average YouNow broadcast is eighteen minutes. If you can stay enthusiastic and upbeat for that long, you'll have no problem doing it in your vlogs lasting less than five minutes.

HOW TO USE YOUNOW TO PROMOTE YOUR VLOGS

When starting off with YouNow, it's advisable to keep a low profile and play around for a couple of weeks until you feel comfortable with the live broadcasting format. For the first fortnight, use YouNow as a way to practise the energy and enthusiasm you need to project in your YouTube videos. Once you've mastered the technique of performing live and keeping people's attention, you'll notice your followers will start to grow. That's when you should announce you have a YouTube channel. Do it when you're starting out and your content isn't up to scratch, and viewers will assume you're using YouNow solely as a means to promote your YouTube channel. Even though you *are* doing this, it shouldn't seem that way to the viewer. The only way they'll engage with you is if they like your content, so if you put your YouTube links up too early, they'll be blind to them when you do start making an impression.

Once your YouNow numbers grow, update your YouNow profile to include a link to your YouTube channel. Make sure the profile box sums up what subjects you vlog about so that people know what to expect. Your live YouNow broadcasts will inevitably be different from your vlogs due to challenges and dares from viewers in the YouNow chatbox, and you don't want viewers going to YouTube and being disappointed. Once a viewer feels let down they won't come back. Be honest and you'll get people who are genuinely interested in the topics you cover. Starting a relationship on an open and honest footing is the way to make it last – on YouNow and in real life.

As you continue to use YouNow, make sure you stay true to your brand values, which you should have written down when you worked through Chapter 1. It's very tempting to respond to all your YouNow viewers' requests, to get more likes and grow in popularity, but you don't want to embarrass yourself and ruin your reputation. Think in advance about where your limits lie. What sorts of things would you never do? Make a list of them and leave the note by the camera that you use to film your YouNow broadcasts.

Also, try to stay as consistent as possible to your vlogging subjects. Aim to talk about subjects that are directly relevant to your vlogs. This is mainly because your YouTube followers will find you on YouNow, and you don't want them to be freaked out by what they see as this could lead to people unsubscribing. Always keep in mind what your YouTube subscribers would think if they saw your YouNow broadcasts. Aim to give them extra content that fits with what you do on YouTube, as they'll think you're boring if you repeat yourself. Be lively and have energy, but keep the core of your operation the same.

PINTEREST
HOW TO INCREASE YOUR PINTEREST FOLLOWERS

Pinterest now beats Twitter as the second-largest driver of traffic from social media accounts to websites and vlogs, according to a recent report by Shareaholic. The company studied thirteen months of data collected from 200,000 publishers reaching more than 250 million unique monthly visitors. Facebook drove the most traffic to those websites, but Pinterest was closely following behind. Technology magazine *Mashable* sums it up by saying: 'When it comes to referral traffic from social networks, there's Facebook and Pinterest – and then there's everyone else.'

While Pinterest consists mainly of sharing images and posts, it also officially supports pinning videos too. As a vlogger you should make use of this feature to encourage others to share both your videos and those made by others in your network. To build a following on Pinterest you should:

OPTIMISE YOUR BOARDS AND IMAGES

In the same way you take time over your YouTube description box using keywords that relate to your niche, you should take care with how you name and describe your Pinterest Boards. Including some keywords in the names of your Pinterest Boards and descriptions of those boards will help people find your videos when they're searching. Remember to also place these keywords in your individual video or image descriptions.

Use the word 'video' in the title name every time you pin a video. This may seem obvious, but often people feel ashamed or silly for using Pinterest for video and don't draw attention to it.

Rest assured that more Pinterest users like video than you think. Even on an image-heavy site like Pinterest, people do search for specific video content and the only way they'll find you is if you make it clear that you have video content.

MAKE YOUR BOARD VISUALLY ATTRACTIVE

You would be amazed at how many people don't think to do this, and just go through the motions of pinning their video content without thinking about what value Pinterest users are getting out of it. Video thumbnails can often look ambiguous and not fully show what's in the video, and if you post a lot of confusing content you won't gain Pinterest followers. Make sure your video thumbnail is attractive and that the board is fleshed out with useful or humorous quotes, and relevant pins. It is important to give your followers something they can visualise in their minds.

If you only pin videos, you are missing out on the greater proportion of people who use Pinterest to view and share images. Think about the subjects your video followers find interesting, and share news articles or infographics that you've found or created.

Think tall not wide when creating your own infographics or posting photos. Because of the way Pinterest is designed, taller and thinner portrait photos work better than landscape ones. The maximum horizontal width is 554 px but there is no limit on vertical height.

THINK THINGS NOT FACES

Social Media agency Curalate examined more than 500,000

images posted by brands to Pinterest, and found that those without faces were more popular with viewers. While this isn't always the case with visual content in social media, the theory holds true for Pinterest. Facebook, for example, is a network of people and Foursquare is a network of places.

'I would have thought that faces make an image more relatable – it's a human seeing a human,' said Curalate CEO Apu Gupta. 'Pinterest is a network of things … and it seems like on a network of things, faces are actually a distraction.' At the time of the study in 2013, less than one-fifth of images on Pinterest included faces. The same study found images with multiple dominant colours have 3.25 times more repins than single dominant colour images, and that images with medium lightness are repinned twenty times more than very dark images. Make sure your photos of things are light and colourful.

MAKE SURE YOUR PIN CONTENT IS USEFUL

Remember the phrase 'less is more'. Although it is important to upload lots of content, potential followers only want useful and decent content. Make sure your pins are relevant to you and your users. What is the subject matter of your vlog? Have that in mind when picking what you pin. Aim to pin images or videos that relate to the content of your vlogs and that sum up what you've been talking about or give extra information about a topic you've recently discussed. Before you pin, ask yourself whether you would click on it or share it if another person pinned it. If the answer is no, then move on and don't pin it yourself as you won't be giving your followers anything useful. That's not to say that you can't throw in the odd random pin you find interesting but, if you want to create a large number of useful followers, then think before you pin!

LINK TO EXISTING SOCIAL NETWORKS

One of the fastest and easiest ways to gain more Pinterest followers is to link to your existing social network accounts. By doing this you will notify your Twitter and Facebook followers that you have pinned something new, thus creating an interest in your account. Since you have already established connections with these social networks, you will grow your Pinterest followers more organically.

UPDATE PINS REGULARLY

In the same way you would update Facebook and Twitter, Pinterest needs to be refreshed just as often. Consistency is important. Aim to update several times in the morning and again in the afternoon.

COMMUNICATE WITH OTHER USERS

If someone likes your pins, like some of theirs back. This will gain you long-term followers and will build up a rapport with people in your niche. The more you give, the more you get.

Actively search for other users like you by using the Pinterest search box. If you're a gaming vlogger, look for other gaming vloggers and experts. Check out related topics as well to find things on computer games, hardware and games brands like Nintendo and Sony. Look at who is pinning these images. Do they have a vlog? If so, they could be vlogging collaboration partners.

If not, the fact that you share a common interest means that they could end up being followers and subscribers – and every follower counts. Try to build up conversations with these other Pinterest users. Start by liking and commenting on their pins and then ask questions about their specialities and why they're interested in specific topics

Follow the Pinterest Boards of brands you've used in your videos, for example fashion retailers or make-up companies. Once they see you're following them, they'll follow you back, and if you've worked with them recently they'll repin some of your content, promoting it to all their followers.

SHARE OTHER VIDEO CONTENT

As Pinterest is based primarily on the concept of sharing (i.e. repinning), you need to make sure that you share other people's images just as much as you post your own. Otherwise you will stand out for being a show-off, and nobody likes a show-off. The most popular Pinterest users repin, like and share other people's pins because that's how these other people discover them. Usually, if someone repins one of your images, you would check out their profile to see who they are and what interests them, and you may follow them back if you have things in common. You can't do this if you use Pinterest only to broadcast what you're doing with your vlog.

The best way to do this is to share content from vloggers who are more popular than you. That way you don't have to be worried that sharing their videos is driving traffic to their YouTube channel, because it's likely your followers are already aware of them.

Pinning helpful and entertaining things – even if they're not your own work – will make your audience see you as an expert and a thought-leader in your field.

HOW TO USE PINTEREST TO PROMOTE YOUR VLOGS

The whole concept of Pinterest is 'sharing', so once you've built up a following by adopting the tips above, you'll find your videos are shared organically. However, it's important to make sure your followers know your great videos aren't just random, and that new content can regularly be viewed on your YouTube channel. The easiest way to do this is with a clear call to action. In your Pinterest descriptions, ask people to share and subscribe to your YouTube channel. They won't think to do it if they're not asked. Pinterest follows the same rule as other social media platforms – whenever you want people to do something, you need to give them clear directions.

Pinterest allows you to customise the design of your account, so make sure it matches the branding you've given to your YouTube channel. Your profile picture should be a good shot of your logo or a related image that's easily recognisable, even in the form of a small thumbnail. You want your viewers to immediately recognise your YouTube channel when they see your pins and comments. Make sure there's a link to your YouTube channel in your profile description, and a note about how regularly you upload new content.

After you've built up a following by creating boards that are a mixture of images and videos, you can create boards that are based solely on videos for organisational purposes. This shows your followers that you have video content, and it's not too self-publicising as the viewers can decide what to watch based on the subjects they're interested in. If you have a beauty vlog channel, for example, you can separate your pins into hair videos, make-up videos, skincare videos etc. Then your viewers will be able to get to the videos they're most interested in more easily. When doing this, it's very important to make sure each video has a unique custom thumbnail that sums up what it's about and looks colourful and cool. The custom thumbnail is what prompts Pinterest users to decide whether or not they want to watch that particular video.

After reading through the tips and tricks in this chapter, you should have a strategy when it comes to:

☐ Facebook
☐ Instagram
☐ Twitter
☐ Vine
☐ Snapchat
☐ YouNow
☐ Pinterest

CHAPTER 8

DRIVING TRAFFIC THROUGH VLOGGER COLLABORATIONS

Before we can hope to make money from vlogging, we need to increase the amount of traffic to our vlogs. The quickest way to do this is to persuade a successful vlogger to mention us or allow us to make a guest appearance in one of their videos. I briefly mentioned collaborations when talking about YouTube in Chapter 6, but they deserve a whole chapter because they can have transformative effects on video views and subscribers.

Collaborations work because when you team up with another YouTuber who has a similar audience, the two of you can each double your reach for at least one video. If that other YouTuber has hundreds of thousands – or even millions – of subscribers, you'll be reaching a lot more people than you would by simply promoting your vlogs on Twitter, Facebook, Snapchat and Instagram.

The world's wealthiest vloggers have made at least one

collaboration video during their career, and most do at least one per month. As an example, here's a list of who's collaborated with whom, along with some background as to how these collaborations came about.

ZOELLA

Believe it or not, Zoella was less famous than her boyfriend Alfie Deyes when they first met. Her earliest collaborations were with her friend Louise Pentland, who has the successful vlog Sprinkle of Glitter.

In August 2012, Zoe and Louise attended the Summer in the City networking convention, where they both queued up to meet Alfie, who was there with his friend Marcus Butler. Zoe had a fan placard saying: 'Dear Alfie and Marcus, I love you so much.' Meanwhile, Louise held a sign saying: 'Dear Marcus/Alfie, marry me, please – Sprinkleofglitter.'

Shortly after this, Zoe asked all her fans to comment on one of Alfie's videos and say 'Zoe sent me'. This attracted Alfie's attention, and the pair started conversing over Twitter. Eventually, they started dating and making videos together. Now they share a £1 million five-bedroom mansion in Brighton, and they appear in a lot of each other's daily vlogs.

ALFIE DEYES

Alfie's first collaborations were with Marcus Butler. Natural pranksters, the pair filmed silly videos together and challenged each other to do bizarre activities, from chest-waxing to smashing eggs in each other's faces.

However, it was fellow YouTuber Caspar Lee who helped to boost Alfie's profile the most. In July 2012, Caspar interviewed a young up-and-coming Alfie for one of his vlogs, and Alfie benefitted from a surge in traffic. As of March 2016, Caspar Lee has 5.7 million YouTube subscribers and Alfie is closing the gap with 4.9 million.

CASPAR LEE

Caspar started off making YouTube videos aged sixteen from the bedroom of his home in South Africa. After launching and failing with two channels, he started up DiCasp (short for Director Caspar) and that took off. He took a risk and travelled to the UK, where he collaborated with Jack and Finn Harries from the Jack's Gap YouTube channel, Marcus Butler and controversial YouTube prankster Sam Pepper.

Now he's moved to London, and the biggest benefit to his traffic has been collaborating with Olajide Olatunji of the YouTube channel KSI. Olajide has a massive 12 million subscribers, lives in a luxury apartment in The Shard and drives a Lamborghini – all paid for with his vlogging earnings. Caspar and Olajide are starring in a humorous feature film in 2016 called *Laid in America*.

JOE SUGG

Not only does Joe benefit from collaborations with his successful elder sister Zoe Sugg, a.k.a. Zoella, but he shares a flat in London with Caspar Lee. The collaborations between Joe and Caspar have been so successful, they've worked together outside of YouTube and earned thousands as a result. They've made a feature film called *Joe & Caspar Hit the Road*, and both voiced animated characters in *The SpongeBob Movie: Fish out of Water*.

MARCUS BUTLER

Marcus and Alfie Deyes have a unique chemistry that makes teenage girls around the world giggle and fall in love, and when they're together they're funnier than when they're on their own. They also share the Guinness World Record for most bangles put onto a wrist in thirty seconds.

However, Marcus's traffic got a real boost when he collaborated with American vlogger Tyler Oakley. Tyler was one of the first YouTube stars, setting up his channel in 2008, whereas Marcus didn't get going until 2010. Tyler currently has 8 million YouTube subscribers, but Marcus is steadily growing and has 4.2 million.

JIM CHAPMAN

Jim and his wife Tanya often do double-date-style YouTube collaborations with Zoella and Alfie Deyes. The four-way collaboration benefits everyone and reflects real life, as couples often hang out with other couples. Audiences like to feel as if their favourite vloggers lead similar lives to them.

Jim has his sisters to thank for his vlogging career: they are Sam and Nicki Chapman, who create YouTube make-up tutorials under the name Pixiwoo. They started in 2008 in the early days of YouTube, and Pixiwoo was one of the first channels to reach 1 million subscribers. Every video they post receives thousands of comments from women around the world thanking them or requesting new videos be made about specific subjects. Sam and Nicki featured Jim in some of their videos, giving him a huge traffic boost at the start of his career.

TANYA BURR

Tanya is married to Jim Chapman, and she also has his sisters to thank for kick-starting her vlogging career. In fact, she piggybacked on the Pixiwoo name when she first launched, and that's why her YouTube channel is called Pixi2woo. Sam and Nicki used her as a model in many of their make-up videos and let her demonstrate some of her techniques, plugging Tanya's channel at every opportunity.

Sam and Nicki were also the first signing to the agency that most UK superstar bloggers are represented by – Gleam Futures – and introduced Tanya and Jim to Gleam.

FLEUR DE FORCE

Fleur Bell is a great friend of Tanya Burr and Jim Chapman, and has appeared on both of their channels. In 2012, she made a comedy video with Tanya where they dressed Jim, and she's also filmed videos with Tanya in which they've applied each other's make-up. Tanya was originally going to do make-up for Fleur's wedding, but attended as a guest in the end due to work commitments getting in the way. Nevertheless, the trio remains close, and the collaboration has helped Fleur to achieve a respectable 1.35 million YouTube subscribers.

HARRY LEWIS

Specialising in videos about FIFA games, Harry has risen to the top ranks of YouTube and his W2S channel is rated 17th most popular in the UK and 153rd most popular in the entire world. This is largely thanks to Olajide 'KSI' Olatunji, who generously welcomed Harry into his gaming syndicate called The Ultimate Sidemen. The Ultimate Sidemen make videos based on group competitions on FIFA video games.

However, Harry also has a bromance with Joe Sugg, and the pair often exchange tweets saying how much they love each other. This inspires each boy's followers to check out the other's YouTube channel.

Why are collaborations so popular? You might wonder why a vlogger with millions of subscribers would help a vlogger with a few subscribers. Louise Pentland from Sprinkle of Glitter explains, saying: 'It's not competitive. It's an all-ships-rise-in-high-tides kind of industry. If I help someone gain subscribers or gain views, it doesn't detract from my success. So it's in everyone's interests to collaborate and work together, which is really nice as that only breeds a positive environment for everyone to work in.'

Collaborations come in several forms – guest appearances, exchanged mentions and joint-effort collaborations. It's important to be clear what type of collaboration you're after before you approach another vlogger to work with. Usually, the type of collaboration you propose will depend on how much of an audience the other vlogger has, whether they cover a similar or different subject matter and whether there's a dramatic difference between you in terms of popularity.

Guest appearances are when one of you appears as a guest in the other's videos and the person that's hosting the video does more work. Usually the host interviews the guest about what they do or asks for their opinions on certain topics. These work well if your audiences might not have heard of the other vlogger, if you cover slightly different subjects or if they've made a popular video recently about a certain subject that you think they'd like to talk about more.

Exchanged mentions are the easiest way to collaborate. In the outro to your video, along with thanking your fans for watching, you give a shout-out to a vlogger that you love and hope they do the same for you. You could say something like: 'If you like this topic as much as I do, check out my vlogger friend!' Then add a link to your friend's YouTube channel in the description or in an annotation link on your video. If they return the mention, you'll both get more views from audience members who are interested in the topic you cover. This is great if you know the other person is busy and may not have time to film a video with you, if you live far away from each other or if you want to start a relationship with a specific vlogger in a gradual way. Rather than committing time and effort to make a video with someone, you can test the waters by seeing if mutual mentions help grow traffic for both of you. If they do, then it's a sign you should do more together.

Joint-effort collaborations are when you work together on a video and then each upload part of the video to your YouTube channel. Then, in the outro, you tempt your audience to go to the other vlogger's YouTube channel. This call to action should contain a reason to watch the rest of the video by giving some hints about what the remaining content is about. These types of collaboration usually work best if you cover similar subjects. Gaming vloggers and cookery vloggers will struggle to find common ground, but two make-up vloggers can each demonstrate techniques on a model – with one vlogger doing eyes and the other doing lips, for example – and the video would be easy to divide up.

With joint-effort collaborations it's very important to lay down some ground rules at the start. This is because you'll be putting a lot of work into the collaboration, so you want to make sure the other person is equally committed. Ask them how and when they want to film the content and where. If they sound vague, try to convince them to agree to specific details, Ask yourself honestly if you see the collaboration working out and don't waste time on it if the answer is no. It's best to accept that the other vlogger may not be your ideal collaboration partner and you should spend time looking for another, rather than chasing someone who's not interested.

Also, be realistic about whom you approach. It may seem logical to attempt to collaborate with vloggers with 50,000 followers or more to give your traffic a significant boost, but you have to ask yourself what the other vlogger is getting out of it. If you were the vlogger with 50,000 subscribers, would you really want to collaborate with someone who had 5,000 or less? Don't be ashamed to aim lower, as it's not just about the numbers you reach; it's also about gaining exposure with a new audience. Even if you're just reaching another 5,000 people, those people may never have discovered you before the collaboration and so it's worth doing. Making ten collaboration videos with vloggers who each have 5,000 subscribers is like doing one with someone who has 50,000. Be prepared to put the work in and do more collaboration videos on a smaller scale, and you'll get the numbers to make bigger vloggers notice you.

**TIP: GO THE EXTRA MILE TO MAKE OTHER
VLOGGERS NOTICE YOU**

Vlogger Roger Xiberras (youtube.com/roger) has appeared in several videos made by successful vloggers. He suggests coming up with a stunt to get noticed, admitting: 'When I first started making videos, I approached all the big names for collaborations – Alfie, Marcus and Jim – and they weren't interested. They didn't think they had anything to gain from working with me, but I knew I had a lot to gain from appearing in their videos.

'I ended up gatecrashing their videos. I'd meet them at events like Summer in the City or smaller vlogger meet-ups, and position myself so that I'd be in the background of a video, holding up a post-it note or a business card with my details on it. I'd also pull a silly face to make the vlogger laugh when they were editing. I did it in a harmless way and most vloggers kept me in their videos. I even built up a reputation and a following for being the guy that keeps appearing in other people's videos, and it attracted more traffic to my YouTube channel. After that, I was able to do more conventional collaboration videos.'

Roger now works full-time filming and directing videos, and you can see some of his work on his website RogStarKid (rogstarkid.com).

Now you know what the three types of collaboration are in theory, how can you make one happen? First, you need to approach potential collaboration partners in the right way. Start by laying the groundwork. Don't be over-friendly too quickly. Think about how friendships develop in real life. You have a chat, then you chat some more and then you might arrange a social event. Building a friendship takes time. The same can be said of vlogging relationships. Start by commenting on the other vlogger's videos and exchanging messages on social media. Once you've established a rapport and been part of each other's lives for a while, the other person will be more open to a collaboration than if you coldly approach them out of the blue.

Secondly, attend vlogger networking events to get to know other vloggers with similar interests and audiences. A lot of vloggers go to events like Summer in the City in a bid to attract the attention of the YouTube superstars. These vloggers are only attending in a bid that their favourite vlogger will notice them, and they are so busy looking up to these famous vloggers that they forget to talk to others on a similar level. Look at who's in the audience of the talks given by your favourite vlogger, because the fact that you've both chosen to attend that talk shows you have at least one interest in common. Talk to as many people as possible, and remember that every conversation will result in at least one new viewer and could lead to more if you end up collaborating.

The American networking event VidCon is the largest meet-up of vloggers in the world, and a great event to attend if you want to appeal to an international audience. Think about the size of America compared to the size of the UK – by collaborating with an American vlogger you could attract millions more viewers. However, don't underestimate the power of the UK's biggest vlogging event, Summer in the City, as several lifelong partnerships have been formed there – including Zoe Sugg's and Alfie Deyes' relationship.

SUMMER IN THE CITY

Summer in the City started in 2009 from humble beginnings and, like YouTube itself, it has spiralled into a massive success, attracting thousands of videomakers from around the world. The numbers were so small at the start that vloggers simply met up in London's Hyde Park. Five years later, 8,000 tickets were sold and the meet-up took over Alexandra Palace. By 2015, the event was so popular that it needed ExCeL in London's Docklands to hold the fans, filmmakers and brands that attended.

The event is run by five friends and YouTubers – Tom Burns, Dave Bullas, Jazza John, Liam Dryden and Luke Cutforth. They all do it on the side of their day jobs and all money goes back into the event. Ticket prices are kept low, and in 2015 it cost just £36 for full weekend access. The YouTube stars who do meet-and-greets and host chats are not paid for their time, doing it simply as a way to give back to their fans and sell merchandise and books.

In recent years there has been a decline in the number of stars attending, due to the fact they don't receive payment. In 2015, Zoella, Tanya Burr, Louise Pentland, Joe Sugg and Alfie Deyes all announced that they wouldn't be attending that year's Summer in the City as they'd set up a rival meet-up called Amity Fest, charging fans £70 to meet them for one hour. Summer in the City founder Tom Burns says booking YouTube stars has become difficult. 'It used to be very much the case that I would contact my friends and ask them to come,' Tom told *TenEighty magazine*. 'Now, as many people are separating their social lives from their professional lives, we find that we have to deal with management a lot more. I think some content creators make a lot of comparisons to other conventions in their mind. They think: "It's like VidCon; you should be paying for our flights and time." I'd love to do that but I can't because we have no money. The only way I could physically pay for flights and time is out of my own money, which I work a day job to earn.'

Using their connections, Tom and his Summer in the City co-founders still put together an impressive list of speakers for their 2015 event including Dan Howell, AmazingPhil, the Saccone-Jolys, Patricia Bright, Carrie Hope Fletcher and Elyar Fox.

However, security is tight. Once you've purchased a ticket for the event, you have to apply to meet your favourite vloggers, and applications are put in a ballot. Only a certain number of ballot-winners will meet each star, and winners must bring their ballot number and ID to gain entrance to the meet-and-greet queue. It is possible to buy a ticket for Summer in the City and fail to win any meet-and-greets in the ballot.

Even if this is the case, it is still worth attending. When Summer in the City first started out, it was just a way for people to meet others with similar interests including a mutual love of YouTube. There were no meet-and-greets in the early days because everyone was on a similar level. People who genuinely liked each other went off and collaborated and hence grew their audience.

Without meet-and-greet distractions, you're able to spend more time looking out for people you like the look of and who are on your level.

Q & A: TOM BURNS

Summer in the City co-founder Tom Burns has a successful YouTube channel and has witnessed the growth of several YouTube stars. He gave these top tips on building a following during a Q&A with *ITV News*:

Q: How can I launch my YouTube channel?

Tom: A simple introductory video is always a good way to start. Introduce yourself, talk about some key interests, what brought you to YouTube etc – anything you find interesting.

Q: How do I grow my channel?

Tom: Upload weekly and keep trying different strands of content until you find something that suits you.

Q: What advice have you got for young vloggers starting?

Tom: Hang in there and keep it up! As long as you're having fun, there's nothing wrong with uploading. Weekly videos tend to do better, so if you have time make sure you give them a go, as it will also help grow your audience.

VIDCON

Like Summer in the City, VidCon started small with a meeting of 1,400 people in the Hyatt Regency Century Plaza hotel in Los Angeles. By 2015, it had grown to a convention of 19,500 at the Anaheim Convention Center, and over 300 YouTube stars performed, created and connected with attendees including

BuzzFeed's Ze Frank, Casey Neistat, Benny Fine, iJustine, Jenna Marbles, Prank vs Prank, Joe Penna (MysteryGuitarMan) and Tyler Oakley. Industry professionals included Yahoo's Katie Couric, YouTube CEO Susan Wojcicki and Vessel founder Jason Kilar.

VidCon 2016 expanded further, to include a new area dedicated to video-gaming at the Anaheim Marriott Hotel next to the Convention Center. Panels and discussions with the best YouTube and digital-video-gamers took place alongside live tournaments and gameplay.

Attending VidCon is a real investment, as tickets are $200 on top of the cost of travel and accommodation. However, if you're serious about vlogging, why not incorporate it into your annual holiday and spend a day at the beach afterwards to wind down after all the networking? You will meet people from all over the world and access amazing workshops full of insider tips and tricks on growing traffic and finding your channel's identity.

In 2015, popular workshops included Expanding Beyond Your Vertical, in which top creators who have moved past their original channels explained how they got their communities to follow them across projects and content styles, and cultivated audiences for their new ventures. Dealing with Criticism suggested ways of learning how to disregard trolls, stay calm and view some comments as genuinely helpful constructive criticism. How to Get Yourself Out There answered questions like: How do you make meaningful connections with other creators? How do you find people to collaborate with? How do you build an audience?

Since VidCon attracts so many thousands of people, it has the most brands on board to make life more fun for visitors. In 2015, Instagram had an emoji-themed giant ball pond to celebrate their new emoji hashtag feature, Nickelodeon had minute-long casting auditions in front of executives in a glass-fronted booth and Taco Bell had props from famous YouTubers' videos, giving people the chance to take photos with them.

VidCon is also attended by multi-channel networks and influencer marketing companies, keen to sign up new vlogging talent. Influencer marketing company Neo Reach attended in 2015, hoping to sign up some popular vloggers to connect to brands. They receive a commission fee from the brands for their efforts. The company was founded by friends Jesse Leimgruber and Misha Talavera, and they have helped make several YouTubers become millionaires while becoming wealthy themselves from the commission. They say: 'Approximately 200 social media influencers have earned over $1 million in the past year, and another 550 earned more than $250,000. Popular YouTubers with 1 million-plus followers can earn as much as $40,000 per video and $5,000 per Instagram post. That money is coming from sponsorships that pay out $0.05 to $0.10 per YouTube view, or $0.15 to $0.25 per Instagram like.' There's money in followers, and those followers are often achieved through collaborations.

Every night, these multi-channel networks and marketing companies host parties. These are great opportunities to meet more vloggers and to get noticed by the marketing executives holding the purse strings. Talk to as many people as possible during the day, and ask the people on the stalls or booths hosted by big brands if they're hosting any parties. You'll stand out for your confidence and if you don't ask, you don't get.

Q & A: HANK GREEN

VidCon was founded by brothers John and Hank Green, who also run the YouTube channel Vlogbrothers. In an interview with *Entertainment Weekly* in July 2015, Hank explained how the event has changed since it started in 2010, and described his plans for the future.

Q: How have you seen things change?

Hank: VidCon's goal has always been to evolve with the industry. Originally, in 2010, the majority of people who were enjoying YouTube videos also participated in the creation culture to some extent. At VidCon back then, people were a little like, 'Can I come to the conference if I don't make YouTube videos?' Whereas now, it is not that way, and of course there's a lot of different demographics. You've got fans and you've got creators and you've got industry professionals, and I've always been excited to just capture whatever it is that's interesting about online video right now. And there's always fascinating things. That enthusiasm from the community has been a driver from the beginning, but now it's a bigger part of the conference, and I love it.

Q: So what's new this year? Is there anything in particular that you're excited about?

Hank: We introduced the creator track in 2015, because VidCon was originally created by creators, for creators – and also for the community and the industry. But my heart is with the creator, because it's how I have had such a cool life and been able to do so many cool things. I want to serve people who want to do that and who are doing that, so we created a specific track for that this year. I think last year some of those people felt kind of out of place, if they weren't in the industry and not interested in paying $500 for an industry pass, but they also didn't see themselves as just a fan. I'm really glad to be giving those people a place to fit in. That's the kind of content that really gets me excited.

Q: So what will the creator track look like? What kind of exclusive panels and content does your creator ticket get you into?

Hank: It's everything from how to think about writing good online video, which is a different task than writing other kinds of media, to how to think about monetisation, how to think about analytics, how to think about audience development. And also there are a ton of new platforms that we can be using. From an industry perspective, you talk about the platforms and you say, what's interesting economically about these platforms? But from a creator perspective, it's a totally different thing. It's like, why do I want to use Vine, why do I want to use Snapchat, why is that different from YouTube, why is it different from Twitter? The landscape remains the same, but the questions you ask about the landscapes differ a great deal when you're sitting at a different perspective.

Hank also said that VidCon was often planned at the last minute, because anything decided in advance would be out of date by the time that the conference took place. As it's centred around online content, it needs to reflect that nature of the content. This means it has to be fresh and current and provide information that consumers can't get from older, more traditional media like television and newspapers. Every time you go to a conference like VidCon, there will be surprises that will benefit you in terms of knowledge or network-building.

The top tip to take away from this chapter is that every little counts. If you don't get noticed by the bigger vloggers, find people who will get back to you. Develop friendships slowly and do things for the other person by mentioning them in your videos and giving them shout-outs on social media. Once people see that you're willing to do things for them, they'll be more likely to put themselves out for you.

After reading this chapter, you should have:

☐ Looked for vloggers with a similar audience to yours
☐ Started to comment on their videos and exchange messages on social media
☐ Worked out what kind of collaborations you want to do
– guest appearances, exchanged mentions or joint-effort collaborations
☐ Booked a ticket for Summer in the City
☐ Had a look at the VidCon website to see what workshops will be on and which YouTubers will be attending. When

you know what's going on, you can work out if it's worth buying tickets, as it could be a worthwhile investment in your future career.

CHAPTER 9

FINDING
SPONSORS

PART I – DIGITAL MARKETING AGENCIES

By now, you've spent a lot of time growing a following. It's time to explore how that audience can make you money.

Thanks to new rules on the labelling of sponsored content, it's easy to see that successful vloggers often make videos advertising certain brands. These videos are either hosted on the vloggers' YouTube channels, where they're seen by anyone who views or subscribes to their channel, or they're hosted on the brands' YouTube channels.

For example, Turkish Airlines recently worked with a number of YouTube stars, such as Caspar Lee, Devin Graham and Damien Walters, on its #fortunetraveller initiative. The project involved flying these stars to Istanbul with just a passport and a bag. Once there, they took part in a traditional Turkish fortune-telling event. They were then sent to one of Turkish Airlines' 260 destinations and recorded their experiences of the flights and destinations for the Turkish Airlines YouTube channel. This campaign attracted a new audience to its YouTube channel as it capitalised on the following of each of the vloggers it hired.

Mattessons is another brand that's recently hired vloggers to help direct traffic to its YouTube channel. Their Fridge Raiders campaign used video-games vlogger Ali-A. He was sent a robot called F.R.H.A.N.K. (which stands for Fridge Raiders Hunger Automated Kit) in a locked cube, and worked with his online community to unlock it by cracking a code. The first video, featuring the unveiling of F.R.H.A.N.K., has had over 900,000 views so far. Over the following months, Ali made videos for Mattessons' YouTube channel, where he worked with his community to personalise the robot and create a cool companion for gaming and snacking.

Beauty vloggers seem to do sponsored content the most regularly. When Unilever launched a channel called All Things Hair in 2014, promoting haircare brands Toni & Guy, Dove and VO5, it hired Tanya Burr and Zoella to create the content. Brands like Superdrug, Lush, L'Oréal, Lancôme and The Body Shop have also hired beauty vloggers to showcase and demonstrate their products.

As a vlogger wanting to monetise your following, you should think about how you can work with brands. Brand deals can be very lucrative for vloggers and result in thousands of pounds for just one video, leading to tens of thousands if it's a long-term partnership. Brands negotiate a rate based on the number of subscribers a vlogger has and the average number of viewers their videos get. As a general rule, vloggers with 1 million subscribers can charge £10,000 per video.

So how can a new vlogger get a slice of the sponsored-content pie? The first – and easiest – way is to use a sponsorship platform or an agency that connects vloggers and brands. The second is to approach the sponsorship department of the company you'd like to partner with directly. Let's start with the platforms and agencies, and I'll cover direct approaches in Part II.

Before we start, it's important to be clear on just what sponsored content involves. If you started a job in real life, you'd probably read the contract carefully to make sure your employer hadn't inserted any clauses you didn't like. If you found any inconsistencies, then you wouldn't sign on the dotted line. Every time you do a sponsored post, you have to abide by Advertising Standards Agency guidelines. You should read these guidelines carefully before doing any sponsored posts so that you know what the terms and conditions are. If you feel that working to these guidelines might cause you to lose viewers, you can decide not to do sponsored posts.

In essence, the new Advertising Standards Agency guidelines state that vloggers must use the word 'advert' in the title or the custom thumbnail of a video whenever they're being paid by a brand to endorse a product. Vloggers must also disclose that it's an advert in the YouTube description box. Therefore, while it might be tempting to do a couple of sponsored videos a week to bring in £10,000 to £20,000, vloggers who do this quickly see their audience start to drop off. Viewers visit YouTube to see people talk honestly about subjects they care about, and selling out to brands is a sign that a vlogger's content is not as authentic as it could be.

The amount of sponsored content you can produce without damaging your viewer-and-subscriber figures depends on how much content you produce a week. If you make a video a day, then you could do a sponsored post every fortnight without much backlash. However, if you make only one video a week, then you should spread out sponsored content every four to six weeks. Of course, there is no limit to how many vlogs you can make if they're hosted on the brand's YouTube channel rather than your own.

TIP: THINK ABOUT HOW THE BRAND FITS WITH YOUR CONTENT, NOT HOW MUCH THEY'LL PAY

Charlie McDonnell from charlieissocoollike explains: 'You could lose your whole YouTube audience in a moment if you decide "I want to talk about this company who I don't really care about, but I just want to get some money." That won't help you in the long run on YouTube.'

SPONSORSHIP PLATFORMS

Signing up to a sponsorship platform or a digital marketing agency will cut down your workload. All you have to do is sign up once and they'll match you to brands that are suitable for your audience.

FameBit is the most popular platform for new vloggers as

it allows you to connect with brands that you might not have considered approaching. As long as you have 5,000 subscribers or more, you can join FameBit and receive alerts each time brands post sponsorship opportunities.

The site's model is pretty simple. Brands post opportunities for vloggers to gain sponsorship on a video-by-video basis or an ongoing basis. Sponsorships start at $100 per video, $90 of which goes directly to the YouTuber chosen. FameBit will take 10 per cent, no matter how much the proposal is worth. Sponsorships may start at $100 but they can exceed $1,000, depending on the size of your audience.

To be considered for sponsorship, you just need to monitor the opportunities regularly. When you see a brand that fits with the ethos of your vlogs or a project that you think you are qualified for, you create a sponsorship proposal and submit that through the platform. Lots of vloggers use FameBit and brands often receive hundreds of proposals, so don't be disappointed if you're not picked straight away. It may even be a good thing, as it means you're free to work with a brand that might be a better fit for you.

Once a proposal is accepted, you'll then discuss the terms of the sponsorship with the brand. They'll leave you to make the video, and you'll be paid 48 to 72 hours after the video has been approved by the brand and published.

The way to find success on FameBit is to perfect your proposal. Tailor it to each brand you apply to. You may think it will save time to write a generic proposal and send it to multiple brands, but the people reading the proposal will always be able to tell that you haven't spent much time on it. This creates a terrible impression.

Brand managers will assume that if you don't take care over your proposal, you don't put much effort into your vlogs either. Therefore, to convince the people reading sponsorship proposals to take you seriously, you need to start your proposal from scratch each time. Research each company to see what they specialise in and look for things they could do better. Then personalise your letters, giving an indication of how working with you can benefit that company. Be as specific as possible so it shows you've done your research. Also, be sure to properly introduce yourself, give a good description of your content and explain your audience demographic; this makes the decision-maker feel like they're getting exposure and value by working with you.

Your proposal should contain some detail about how you plan to use their product in your video. Paint them a picture so they can visualise how their brand will be portrayed on screen. Give them links to other videos you've made that have a similar format. Remember, brands are making a leap of faith when they decide to work with a vlogger for the first time. They trust you with their product and vision in the hope that you will love it just as much as they do. Make it as easy as possible for them to imagine what their product would look like on screen if you got the job.

Since you don't want to overload your YouTube channel with sponsored posts, it's important to carefully select specific brands to work with rather than sending out proposals to everyone. Not only is it time-consuming to draft proposals from scratch, but it's a complete waste of effort to approach brands you have nothing in common with. Think about your audience. The brands sponsoring videos on FameBit are doing so because they want to gain more exposure with their target audiences. If your audience doesn't match a brand's target audience, then it may not be the best fit for you. Also, think about whether you actually like the brand enough to recommend it to your audience. If not, move on. You don't want to damage your reputation by plugging a product that leaves your audience feeling disappointed when they try it. Your audience will lose trust in you and this will lead to a decline in subscribers and viewers.

Q & A: ADAM HENDLE

Adam Hendle is Community Director at FameBit. Here, he explains to Vlognation how to use the platform and gives tips about how to make money from it.

Q: How can YouTubers and vloggers use FameBit to increase their revenue?

Adam: Most YouTubers and influencers cannot survive on what they are paid via AdSense for their views. Sponsorships pay much higher and allow YouTubers to find products that they think their audience will love and relate to, which creates great content as well as helps them monetise.

Q: What tips would you give to creators interested in submitting proposals to brands on FameBit?

Adam: The three biggest tips I could give would be to do your homework on the brand, find the right fit for your channel and provide details on how you see the video coming together.

Brands are looking for YouTubers that show genuine interest in their products and have done a bit of digging into their companies. Also, only apply for opportunities that will make sense for your channel. While the allure of getting paid for a sponsorship may seem enticing, you only do damage to your channel if you accept something that isn't a fit. Lastly, make sure to paint the brand a picture of what you plan on doing for them.

Q: Are vloggers able to use multiple video formats and be creative when working with brands?

Adam: We've pretty much seen everything, from hauls, tutorials, look books, skits, reviews etc. What we like to stress to the brand hiring is let the YouTuber be themselves and do what they believe will resonate most with their audience.

Q: FameBit has a referral programme for creators. Could you explain a bit how that works?

Adam: We love our community of YouTubers and we want to reward them for having them help us spread the word. We found the best way to do this was a point-reward system, in which a YouTuber receives 200 points for referring a fellow YouTuber.

We also give one point for every dollar that a YouTuber gets hired for on the platform. For example, if a YouTuber is hired for $200 we give them 200 points. Points can be redeemed for lighting equipment, microphones, cameras and more. The idea is that as you grow your channel, you need better equipment, and we wanted to help make that happen.

DIGITAL MARKETING AGENCIES

Digital marketing agencies are hired by brands to connect them with relevant vloggers. Have you ever been contacted by one? If not, you need to get in contact with these agencies to tell them about your vlog. When you have 5,000 subscribers, get online and type 'digital marketing agencies' into Google. Have a look at each agency's website to see what they do and which brands they work with. If you feel like you'll be a good fit based on their previous work, then phone them. Explain what you vlog about and how much traffic you get.

Often, vloggers let pride get in the way of making money. They assume that if an agency wanted to work with them, the agency would find them. They wrongly think that if they're not being approached it's because they're not good enough. Usually this isn't the case. These digitalmarketing agencies already work with a lot of popular vloggers. When a deal comes up, they turn to those they've worked with previously as it's less of a risk. As they're so busy negotiating deals for these vloggers, they don't always have time to look for new talent. Therefore, you need to be proactive and alert them to your presence.

Eight&four is one of the most well-known digital marketing agencies in the UK and has connected vloggers with brands like Sea World, Velcro and Me By Melia hotels. These deals can be worth thousands to tens of thousands of pounds, depending on how much coverage the vlogger gives the brand. A product mention or recommendation in a video could earn a vlogger in the region of £4,000 whereas a month-long banner advert on a vlogger's YouTube channel could earn that vlogger as much as £20,000.

Eight&four's Managing Director Kate Ross encourages all vloggers to put themselves out there. She told *The Guardian*: 'Approach digital agencies and say, I've got this audience, is there anything you can do with it?'

When approaching a digital agency, make sure you do your research. Find out which brands they've previously worked with and show off your knowledge by writing a carefully-tailored pitch. Summarise your vlog's audience and demographic and explain the type of topics you cover in your videos.

When explaining your demographic, use the data you can find in your YouTube Analytics reports. The three most important statistics to give are age, gender and geographical location, as this is what agencies look for when matching you up with brands. This should go at the very beginning of your proposal. Next, hook the agencies in further by giving them a figure for your audience size per video, or average views per video. As a rule of thumb, look at your five most recent videos and calculate the average views per video. That number is more useful to agencies than your subscriber number, because brands are only interested in how many people will watch the video that they sponsored. So although subscriber count is a shortcut number that identifies how popular your channel might be, it's not always an accurate indication of how many people will actually watch your video.

TIP: LOVE WHAT YOU DO!

As you start to sell your vlog to advertisers, it can be disheartening if you're not getting much attention at first. Don't let this get you down! Remind yourself why you started vlogging. You need to stay enthusiastic so you can grow your traffic and show off an impressive growth rate to advertisers when you speak to them again.

Eight&four's Kate Ross told *The Guardian*: 'If you try to set up a channel or blog just to make money, it's not going to work. It needs to be organic and start with a passion. If it's something you love, it shows.'

When a digital marketing agency or a sponsorship platform matches you with a brand, remember that you are not obliged to take the deal unless you fully believe it fits with your vlog's image and branding. You will lose traffic if you advertise something that goes against your principles, and therefore you'll miss out on money in the long term if you pick the wrong sponsored posts.

Patrick Walker is CEO of business video company Rightster and was previously responsible for launching YouTube in Europe. He's aware of how lucrative it can be to do sponsored posts for brands, yet he advises caution, telling the the *Daily Mail*: 'Every case is unique, but generally video bloggers and other social media stars have opportunities for income that can scale rapidly with the size of their audience on YouTube, Facebook, Twitter and now other platforms like Snapchat. It could be a couple of hundred pounds, tens of thousands of pounds or maybe more depending on who they are, what you ask them to do and the size of their audience on various platforms.

'In the case of YouTube stars, many are getting more than double what they might earn purely on YouTube through advertising from direct brand partnership deals.

'For most of these creators, maintaining their hard-built audiences authentically is a key priority, and we see cases regularly of YouTube stars turning down relatively simple jobs in the tens of thousands of pounds for just a day's work out of principle or disagreement on the creative ask or the brand's interest to them.'

Vloggers like KSI, Zoella, Tyler Oakley and Jenna Marbles receive several approaches every single day from brands wanting to work with them, and they choose less than one a week. This means they could be turning down up to £50,000 each week. If they can refuse that amount of money because they see the benefit in staying true to their audience's values, so can you. It's important to do sponsored posts to earn money, but don't get greedy as it won't benefit you in the long term.

After reading Part I, you should have:

☐ Read the Advertising Standards Agency guidelines on sponsored posts
☐ Signed up to FameBit
☐ Browsed FameBit to see what opportunities are available
☐ Understood the importance of tailor-making a proposal to each brand you approach
☐ Researched digital marketing agencies
☐ Approached digital marketing agencies

* * *

PART II – HOW TO APPROACH BRANDS

After you've been vlogging for a while, you might find yourself mentioning the same brands over and over again. Would you like to earn money from those mentions? Of course you would! Alternatively, you might be aware of new brands launching in your niche, like new fashion stores or a new tech gadget. How do you fancy getting paid for helping them grow by mentioning them to your audience?

If you're not being introduced to the brands you want to work with through a digital agency and their ads are not popping up on platforms like FameBit, then you need to be proactive. You need to submit a sponsorship proposal to the marketing or PR department of the brand you want to work with.

You only get one chance to make a good first impression with your proposal, so it's important to take time over it. This chapter contains a list of the elements that winning proposals should have in them – don't send yours off until you have included every statistic and detail listed.

Before you start approaching brands, get organised. It's useful to make a list of brands you want to approach and then you can tick things off as you make progress. Sponsorship is very much a numbers game. You'll be contacting two types of brands: those who are interested in sponsoring a YouTube channel and those who aren't. You need to email a lot of brands to increase your chances of finding some in the interested category.

Brainstorm a list of every type of product and service that

relates to or complements your videos. For example, lipstick, mascara, face wash, hair and beauty salons and hair products. Once complete, write down brand names next to the products and services on your lists. For example, L'Oréal, Maybelline, Rimmel, Simple and Toni & Guy. Take out different-coloured pens: choose one colour to signify local brands, one for nationals and one for internationals. Mark a dot next to each brand name to help you keep track of whether it's local, national or international. Your list should include all three types.

While national and international sponsors may have deeper pockets, they often place their online advertising through an agency. You may find local and regional sponsors are easier to contact, as you could stop by your local hairdresser or visit a flagship store and ask directly for the person in charge of marketing.

TIP: MAKE THE LIST OF POTENTIAL BRAND PARTNERS AS LONG AS POSSIBLE!

The more potential sponsors you have on your list, the more chance you have of getting a deal. If you feel like your list isn't long enough, try working through these steps:

Step One: Look at which adverts are being sold by YouTube on your vlog – either as in-video ads or as a pre-roll. It's worth adding these companies to your list as they clearly have a budget and you could give them a better deal than YouTube.

Step Two: Look at other vlogs in your niche and see if any companies are advertising on them. If they're advertising on another vlog, then they clearly value the importance of online advertising in principle.

Step Three: Visit industry events and trade fairs and look at the companies who have paid for display stands. If they're paying out for a stand at a trade fair, they're clearly trying to reach more people.

Step Four: Look back over some recent videos and work out what kind of products you have talked about. Who makes these products? Add these brands to your list. Have you ever written about any venues (shops, restaurants, tourist attractions)? If so, add these to your list too. It shows there is a good fit between your viewers' interests and the brands' products or services.

Once you have a list, you should spend time researching each company in more detail. You may find it's not as good a fit as you thought, in which case you can cross it off. Or you may find information that causes you to like it more, and you can use this information when pitching. You should find out:

What is the brand currently doing in video and what could you do that is different? Find the brand's YouTube channel, and look at how many views per video it gets and how many subscribers it has. Could you offer the brand more than it has already? What are its social media figures like? When you're pitching, you need to quote these statistics and suggest how you can grow these figures.

What are the goals the brand is trying to achieve? Has the brand recently launched a new product? Is there a social media platform like Snapchat or Instagram that it's yet to join? Is it lacking great video content? Find out what its weak spots are, and then you can work out ways to solve its problems.

Who is the brand's core audience? Look for interviews that marketing managers have given to media outlets, or articles written about the company, to find out whom it sells the most products to. Look at its products and work out what age range they're targeted at. You can often tell this by looking at packaging and price points.

Are you going to be able to help the brand achieve its goals? Think long and hard about this one. Will a mention in your vlog direct traffic to its site or will you need to do something more creative? You know your audience – do you think they'll really be interested in the brand you're approaching? This is important because happy brands will come back for more. The people at those brands might tell friends who work for other brands. However, unsatisfied customers will never return and it's a lot of work to keep getting new sponsors because unhappy ones have left.

Do you know how to gather the data to make a report once the sponsored activity is over? Educate yourself on the best way to capture figures of social outreach and invest in some data-presentation software. For a brand to be happy, it needs to clearly see results.

CASE STUDY: VINCENT HAYWOOD

Vincent Haywood, Head of Digital at the PR company Shine Communications, often uses vloggers to promote brands.

Talking about his experience working with vloggers to the *Daily Mail*, Vincent said:

'We've used vloggers in a number of campaigns for our clients, their influence is phenomenal. Be it a small mention of a product, or a fully-fledged interview regarding a brand, we have seen a massive spike in traffic or sign-ups.

'One campaign we worked on included a pre-campaign teaser by Zoella, and the teaser – not even the full campaign, just a teaser – saw our subscribers grow by over 5,000 per cent. That clip was sixty seconds long.

'Vlogger PewDiePie makes an estimated £2.5 million a year in advertising revenue alone; that's without what he charges for mentions or game reviews. For a top-tier vlogger, you are looking at anything from £20,000 to £50,000 for a five-minute video. If we choose the right vlogger and the right content, we are guaranteed fantastic results. That is money well spent.'

In short, brands are willing to pay huge amounts if you prove that you can drive traffic to their websites and social media channels.

THE ELEMENTS OF A WINNING PROPOSAL

To help you remember what to include in a great proposal, think of the phrase 'Positive Mental Thoughts – Boom!' The four elements needed for any proposal begin with the letters P, M, T and B, and if you get it right, then you'll see your finances skyrocket. Boom!

P IS FOR... PERSONALISED EMAIL

It's very important to write a proposal tailored to each brand. Use the research that you did when working out whether the brand was a good fit for you or not.

The best way to approach a brand is by email, so you can explain clearly what you're offering. Also, it enables the brand manager to read it at their convenience. When you're telephoning someone, it's on your terms and you have no idea if the other person is in a mood to listen.

The subject line of your email is vital, as this will determine whether people are enticed to open your email or not. You should spend almost as much time thinking up a subject line as you do picking titles for your vlogs. You should aim to tease the sponsorship department into opening your emails by summing up your vlog content and personalising it to the brand. For example: 'Introducing [insert subject] Vlogger [insert your name] / Working With [insert brand name].'

Next, make sure you address the email to a person, and not send an email that consists of 'info' or 'enquiries' in the address. Emails sent to addresses that start with 'info' or 'enquiries' often slip through the system and don't get read by anyone. You'll have put time into your proposal, so it's worth putting in a bit more extra time to find a real email address so the proposal will be read. If contact details for humans can't be found on the brand's website, then call up and ask. You could also do some research using LinkedIn. Once logged into LinkedIn, use its search facility to search for the brand and refine the search by location, e.g. UK or US. This should bring up a long list of people who work for that company, and you can go through that to find someone in charge of marketing. Don't rule out using your social media network to ask if anyone knows someone who works for that brand. It's all about getting your foot in the door, and that means finding the right person to read your email.

Be as concise as possible. Brand managers are busy, so you must make it easy for them to understand what you want and how it can benefit them. Just like with your vlogs, keep your proposal short and sweet. Every sentence should be full of details and specifics. Tell them about your vlog and what you can help them with. Include these details: Who is your audience? How many average views per video do you get? Tell them why you chose to contact them and what problems you can help the brand with.

When you sign off, add more intrigue and anticipation by saying you could send all your statistics in a media kit if they're interested. Close the email with a signature containing all your contact information. Also include a link to your YouTube channel and blog, if you have one.

Here is an example showing how you could put all these points together:

Hi [Name],

I run a [vlog subject] vlog at [YouTube channel URL]. I have [statistic] average views per video, [statistic] subscribers and [statistic] Twitter / Instagram / Facebook followers interested in [subject].

I am contacting you to see if you would be interested in advertising on my YouTube channel. I have noticed that [fact about the company] and I could offer you some highly targeted traffic to [how you can help the brand achieve one of its goals].

Let me know what you think. I am looking forward to hearing from you. If you have any questions, then don't hesitate to ask, and I can send you a media kit with all my vlog's statistics if required.

Yours,

[Your Name and contact details]

Remember that you won't get positive responses from everyone, and it's important not to let negative responses slow you down or distract you. There are lots of reasons why a brand could be uninterested. It could be the wrong time of year for its advertising budget, or it may not currently be focused on online advertising. Keep your head high, watch some of your videos to remind yourself why you do what you do and approach more of the brands on your list.

M IS FOR... MEDIA KIT

You don't need a media kit when you send off your initial email, but you need to have it prepared so you can send it as soon as a brand asks for it. Some brands may get back to you fairly quickly, and media kits take a long time to prepare. You don't want to rush them, nor do you want to keep the brand waiting as this destroys the momentum of your dialogue. They've requested the media kit because they're interested right now. Keep them waiting and they could change their minds!

A media kit should contain:

Current headshot: As a vlogger, you are the face of your brand and it's important to give advertisers an idea of what they are buying into. You may think that anyone who watches your vlogs will know what you look like, but don't assume advertisers have watched any of your videos. You need to convince them to visit your channel with a knock-out media kit, and a photo is an important part of that. Show them how presentable you are by making sure that the photograph is well-lit and your face is clearly visible.

Your bio: Advertisers read through hundreds of pitches a week. The difference between the successful ones and the rejected ones depends on how quickly the advertiser can understand the concept of a brand. Aim to sum up in one sentence what your vlog is about and how you can be useful to the advertiser. Follow that by explaining why your vlog is unique and different to others, to persuade the advertiser there's a benefit to working with you rather than other vloggers who cover a similar subject matter. Don't waffle and don't make this explanation longer than four sentences.

Channel traffic statistics: Ultimately, advertisers make decisions based on numbers. They want to see how many people they could reach by placing an advert on your vlog. Use your YouTube Analytics figures and share your channel's average views per video and subscriber numbers. You could also share the average viewing time per video if it's more than a couple of minutes long, as this demonstrates that your viewers stick with you until the end of a video and indicates to advertisers your viewers are highly influenced by you. Advertisers are looking for influencers as viewers are more likely to buy from vloggers they're inspired by than by vloggers whose videos bore them after less than a minute.

Social media presence: This is the place to show off your social media popularity. Hopefully, you'll have followed the tips in Chapter 7 and have grown your audience on Facebook, Twitter,

Instagram and Snapchat. Remember that most ordinary people struggle to reach just a few hundred followers, so if you have a thousand followers or more on any social media platform you have a right to show off! Social media is a further indication of how influential you are, as it shows that your audience has made an effort to follow you outside of the YouTube platform. Advertisers like to know that you have reach because they want you to tease links to videos containing one of their adverts on social media and they want to feel confident that you have the network to make people aware of their product.

Viewer demographics: Advertisers need to know who's watching your vlog and where your traffic is coming from geographically. This is because they are aiming their products at a specific demographic and they want to see whether your audience fits into that demographic. For example, if your viewers were all aged eighteen to thirty and based in the UK, then you wouldn't be a good fit for advertisers marketing American-manufactured hearing aids. However, you might be a good fit for beauty or fashion advertsing. Use your YouTube Analytics figures to share where your audience is based geographically, gender distribution and age distribution.

Press clippings or media features: If you've caught the attention of a local or national newspaper, a TV channel or a magazine, then boast about it. This shows advertisers that you have a reputation as an expert in your field. When there are lots of people vlogging about the same subject matter, the fact that a media outlet chose to feature you sets you apart from the crowd. If you haven't been featured in any publications yet, then simply leave this part out of the media kit. Nobody will judge you for a lack of press clippings, as these will come in time.

Awards, honours and other testimonials: Has your vlog won any awards? Have you been nominated or shortlisted for anything yourself? This could help to swing the balance in your favour if an advertiser is unsure about whether to work with you or not. If you are yet to receive recognition for your vlog, then don't worry. You can use this section to feature two or three testimonials about your vlog. Ask experts and industry leaders to watch your vlogs and give you positive feedback, and use their quotes here. The right testimonials can be as powerful as an award. For example, if you're a fashion vlogger, then a testimonial from a *Vogue* magazine fashion editor would show you had credibility and make your vlog seem like a trustworthy, reputable resource.

Current, accurate contact information: Make it easy for advertisers to say yes! They don't have time to search through a long document for your contact information. Have it at the top of every page of your media kit so it's easy for them to locate immediately.

Once you have a media kit you can put it online, and you may find that you start to receive approaches from brands you might not have considered contacting. This is because having a media kit is a sign that you take advertising – sometimes you need to spell it out for brands. If you have a blog connected to your vlog, then make sure your blog contains an 'advertise here' link somewhere on the homepage. This 'advertise here' link should take people to a page of your blog that hosts the media kit. If you don't have a blog, you could upload a portion of your media kit to your Facebook page and let people know they can contact you to receive the whole thing.

T IS FOR... TELEPHONE CALL

A mistake many vloggers – and bloggers – make is they assume one approach by email is enough. In the technology-obsessed world we live in, having a phone conversation is something a lot of people are frightened of. These people are missing out on potential advertisers... and money. Brands need to be chased if they don't reply to you. You deserve a yes, no or maybe.

When calling, think about your own working day. Would you like to receive a phone call at nine o'clock in the morning when you're sorting your desk out and sipping your first coffee of the day? Probably not. But how about after lunch, when you've made some progress on your 'to do' list and hence you're less likely to snap at anyone who disturbs you? Between 2pm and 3pm is a good time to call.

All you need to do is introduce yourself, ask if they received your email and sound happy. Enthusiasm is infectious, so if you're positive they're more likely to be positive back. They'll either say that they're interested and want more details, so you can send them a media kit, or they'll say no. Always ask the reason for a no, so that you know how to modify your behaviour or channel and try again when you think the situation has changed. And don't lose heart when you get nos. Just get back to your list, and work through the brands until you find a yes. Someone out there needs you. And remember that if you're getting rejections from large companies, aim smaller.

B IS FOR...BE PREPARED FOR A YES!

It's easy to become so fixated on the proposal that you forget you'll have more work to do when potential brands show interest. You are responsible for closing the deal. When a potential advertiser has replied to you saying that they are interested, you have to take that drop of interest and whip it up so it becomes a huge bowl of excitement.

In your next communication with the brand, be prepared to suggest meeting face to face. This allows you to test the waters. If a brand is very interested in you, they'll make time to meet, but if they're not yet sold they might delay. That's fine. Send them an impressive media kit and then they'll make time in their schedule for you.

Plan what you would wear to this meeting as it's vital to look smart and professional. When an advertiser is sponsoring your vlog, they are also sponsoring your personality, so you need to be a good ambassador for your vlog.

Work out your pricing structure and practise delivering it in a confident way. If you sound unsure when you ask a brand to part with money, it will make them unsure about spending it. Remind yourself of how many viewers your vlog gets and how the brand could improve in certain areas. This advertiser needs you!

Work out different prices for different tasks. You would charge more for a whole video based around a brand than you would do for a mention in one of your top five or haul videos. If you have a blog related to your vlog, think about how much you could charge for a mention or blog post. Giving an advertiser a list of options makes them feel more in control, as they can choose what to buy based on their budget.

You'll make more money if you price the video low and charge extra for add-ons. For example, you could say that a video is £500, then an extra £200 to promote it on Instagram or £300 to publicise it on all your social networks. When you're offering this, have the figures for your social media followers to hand so it looks more appealing to the brand.

Don't be greedy at the start. While you may have heard statistics of established vloggers earning up to £5,000 for a sponsored vlog, you need to be realistic when you're new. Start off by putting together a package – consisting of the video and add-ons – worth £500 to £1,000, depending on the size of the brand. If it's a big brand, then go for the higher figure, as selling yourself too cheaply will devalue your hard work. For a big brand, £500 is pocket change, and it won't appreciate what it's getting for its money. However, when it spends £1,000 on a project, it'll feel like it's made more of a commitment and get more involved. For a local brand, £500 is an investment, so adjust your prices accordingly and don't price yourself out of its league. Having sponsors on board, even if they're not paying much, will help you attract other sponsors who will pay more. No brand likes to take risks and be the first to do something. Once you've shown you can make videos for some businesses, others will want you too.

As soon as a brand has confirmed what package it wants, make sure you give your contact clear payment terms and conditions. After all, you're doing it because you want to get paid. The usual payment method involves a vlogger sending an invoice to the brand once the video is up, and then setting a date on which they expect payment. As a rule, tell brands that you expect payment within thirty days of invoicing, and ask if they have a problem with that. It's not unusual for brands to ask for 120 days between invoicing and payment, and if that's the case you both want to be clear about that in advance. You may get them to make the payment sooner – if you don't ask, you don't get!

TIP: SET UP A BUSINESS BANK ACCOUNT AND SORT OUT YOUR TAX ARRANGEMENTS

Don't forget that you have to pay taxes on what you earn. Vlogging is a business, and you have to pay tax on your profits just like any other business. When you start to get an audience, remember that the taxman is one of the people watching you and you will get found out if you try to keep all your earnings for yourself.

The easiest way to get started is to notify HMRC that you would like to go self-employed, which means registering as a sole trader. There is minimal paperwork and you don't have to pay company formation costs. All you need to do is register online at the Sole Trader's section of the HMRC website (gov.uk/set-up-sole-trader). Then you're responsible for completing a Self Assessment tax return each year and for paying National Insurance.

Once you start to bring in more money, you'll find it's more efficient to set up a limited company. Not only does this look more professional when sending invoices to advertisers, but it will bring in more money after tax.

Limited companies are subject to corporation tax of 20 per cent no matter how much they make, and you will be liable for fewer National Insurance contributions if you take your earnings in dividends. Another advantage is that you can easily bring in investors or partners at a later date by selling shares in the limited company. You can set up a limited company for as little as £15 by simply registering at Companies House (.companieshouse.gov. uk//runpage?page=welcome). However, it is advisable to hire an accountant when you set up a limited company, as there are responsibilities to file a Company tax return with HMRC and a Company annual return at Companies House. An accountant will save you time so you're free to do what you do best, earning money through making videos; they should save you some cash as they know all the benefits open to limited companies. When you have a steady stream of income, start to look for an accountant.

No matter what scheme you choose, you should set up a separate bank account. If you're a sole trader, you have to open up a separate current account, as business bank accounts require a company formation number that only limited companies have. It's worth doing because it helps keep your finances organised. Put all your money in your regular bank account and you'll be tempted to spend everything you earn. Plus you can use the money from the second bank account to finance new camera and editing equipment and pay for other vlogging costs.

When you register a limited company, you are legally

obliged to open a business bank account, as a limited company is regarded by the law as a distinct entity and must be kept separate from your own affairs. Visit a money advice website like Money Saving Expert (moneysavingexpert. com) or Money Facts (moneyfacts.co.uk) and search for their business banking comparisons to get a good deal. Banks will charge you a monthly fee for a business bank account, but these price comparison websites contain a list of deals such as fee-free banking for an introductory period. They also list how much each bank charges a month so you can pick one with a low rate.

After reading Part II, you should have:

☐ Created a list of brands to approach
☐ Divided the list of brands into local, national and international targets
☐ Researched each company on the list to work out how you could help them
☐ Memorised the elements of a winning proposal: Positive Mental Thoughts – Boom!
☐ Registered with HMRC as a sole trader or limited company
☐ Set up a separate bank account

CHAPTER 10

WORKING WITH TALENT MANAGERS

When you're ready to earn money outside of YouTube through sponsored vlogs and brand endorsements, talent managers make life a lot easier. They find the brands for you, they negotiate the highest-possible prices because they receive commission relative to what you earn, and they draw up the contracts. This leaves you free to focus on what you're best at – making great content!

Finding a manager can be tricky because they'll only sign you up if you have a following. Without subscribers, brands won't offer you sponsored-content deals and therefore the talent managers won't receive any commission. The better-known the talent agency, the harder it is to join. That's because these managers are already working with vloggers who earn a lot of money. You need to persuade them that you have what it takes to be commercially successful.

Take a look at the number of subscribers to your YouTube channel and be honest with yourself. You don't need a million subscribers before you can realistically expect a manager to sign you up, but you should have at least 10,000 and proof that this figure is constantly growing.

If your subscriber numbers aren't what they should be, you need to put more work into growing your audience. Re-read the first few chapters of this book to make sure you're clear about your image and brand, and set some targets for traffic growth. Re-read the chapters on growing your audience to make sure you're reaching out to other vloggers and attending networking events like Summer in the City and VidCon. The bosses of the major talent agencies also give some advice to new vloggers below – take note and act on their advice before you approach them. Be prepared to put in the work to grow your numbers. Success does not happen overnight, but it can happen if you work methodically and put the hours in. Dominic Smales is the founder of the UK's largest vlogging talent company, Gleam Futures, and, as he explained to CNN, a lot of work goes into being successful: 'This is something these guys have been working on for years, making content tirelessly in their bedrooms.

'People are now suddenly taking notice and saying: "Oh my God, look at the overnight success this girl has achieved," but it's not – it's years of toil.'

Once you've grown your subscriber numbers, get clued up on which talent agencies exist and find out what they can offer you. Their websites might also contain some information about how you can apply. Learning as much as you can about these companies, like what other vloggers they represent, how they started out and what brands they've worked with, will help you pitch. You want to prove that you complement their existing line-up and that you are passionate about their agency in particular. I've put together guides on the biggest talent agencies in the UK – Gleam Futures, Mode Media and OP Talent – as well as the leading agency in the US – Addition. Below is a basic guide to each, and I strongly recommend that you do some additional research by visiting each company's website.

GLEAM FUTURES

Gleam was founded in 2010 by Dominic Smales. He initially envisioned his company being a social media consultancy advising brands how to operate on YouTube, but he ended up taking vloggers under his wing. The company now describes itself as a 'social talent management agency' on its website (gleamfutures.com).

The shift in business came about when he noticed some early vlogs made by Sam and Nicki Chapman, a.k.a. Pixiwoo, and signed them up. At the time, the most popular videos on YouTube tended to be of singing dogs or crashing Ferraris, but whenever Sam and Nicki posted a video, it made the Top 5 or Top 10 list of the most viewed videos of the day. Dominic spotted how much traffic they were getting and saw a money-making opportunity.

After he had signed the Pixiwoo sisters, he wasted no time in finding them endorsement deals. Their first one was with make-up brush brand Real Techniques. It proved a success for all parties as it became the fastest-growing brush brand in the US within five years. In the UK, Real Techniques' brushes now account for 60 per cent of the market share, on a par with established brands like MAC and Laura Mercier.

Today, Dominic and a team of thirty Gleam talent managers represent some of the most popular British vloggers, including Zoe and Joe Sugg, Alfie Deyes, Tanya Burr, Jim Chapman, Niomi Smart and Caspar Lee. He expects their careers to grow even bigger in coming decades. 'We're not in the business of having one-hit wonders or trying to monetise them aggressively over the next two years,' he said in an interview with the *Financial Times*. 'I feel an almost paternal, personal responsibility to make sure they have a really great long career, because that's what we are in for.'

Gleam's talent roster: Zoe 'Zoella' Sugg, Alfie Deyes, Joe Sugg, Jim Chapman, Tanya Burr, Louise Pentland, Marcus Butler, Caspar Lee, Ruth Crilly (A Model Recommends), the Saccone-Jolys, Lily Pebbles, Niomi Smart, TheLeanMachines, Samantha Maria (Beauty Crush).

Gleam's brand deals: Gleam have matched Tanya Burr with Scholl, Superdrug, Specsavers, The Body Shop and VO5; Zoella with Unilever, Topshop and Lush; Joe Sugg with Tesco Mobile, Coca-Cola and Skype; Caspar Lee with O2 and Turkish Airlines; Alfie Deyes with HTC and Bestival; Marcus Butler with Samsung; Jim Chapman with Hudson Boots, River Island and TK Maxx; Louise Pentland with very.co.uk and Coca-Cola; Samantha Maria with Fujifilm and New Look; and Niomi Smart with bareMinerals and L'Oréal.

Gleam founder Dominic Smales' advice: Put yourself out there – 'Gleam looks for talent, not subscribers, when signing new vloggers. We take people who we think are brilliant. They might have just three subscribers or they might have 300,000 – what we're looking for is enthusiasm, a great personality, high production values and an ability to relate to people. We like to take people at one stage of their career, work with them and create opportunities for them. We welcome applications from anyone who is enthusiastic about what they do.'

Collaborate – 'Collaborate with other vloggers and share their content. Mention other vloggers that you like in your videos. Make sure to collaborate with all platforms – work with TV stations and magazines to get your content out there. Also, use social media in a sociable way to talk to other vloggers and interact with people. If you're just using social media to shout about new content, then that won't go down well.

Love what you do – 'You have to be extremely passionate, because to be successful you have to live and breathe it and be incredibly tenacious. Success doesn't happen straight away and you have to enjoy it enough to keep going at the start when you're not making any money from it. This could be as long as four years. Also, if you love what you do, you're more likely to have some expertise in it, and that's important as viewers like to learn something through watching videos.'

Be true to yourself – 'Don't try to copy other vloggers. Just be yourself and you'll come across as genuine and authentic and therefore likeable.'

MODE MEDIA

Mode, formerly known as Glam, started in 2004 by matching brands with bloggers and online digital-content creators. In 2004 it had just twelve content creators, but as of 2016 that number stood at 6,000 and included video creators as well as bloggers.

Mode acquires talent from all niches including women's style, fashion, beauty, men's lifestyle, health and wellness, parenting, food, entertainment and music. Once they've signed you up, they'll heavily promote you on Mode.com – an online platform for the best of their content creators, which reaches a whopping 25 million monthly users.

Mode Media's talent roster: Cassey Ho (Blogilates), Michelle Phan, Dani Spies and Steve Booker.

Mode Media's brand deals: Mode has matched Cassey Ho with Jamba Juice, Reebok, GNC and Quest Nutrition; Michelle Phan with Lancôme, Random House and L'Oréal; and Steve Booker with PayPal.

Mode Media's Izan Nash's advice: Be versatile – 'Before recruiting vloggers, I have to assess in which areas – be it fashion, beauty, family, food or men's lifestyle etc. – the company requires influencers for upcoming campaigns. Talented people with versatile interests, who cover a range of topics, are ideal because their audiences are really receptive to a varied range of content. That said, it's good for a vlogger to be an expert in one particular field, and many start out focusing on just one area before branching out.'

Develop a loyal audience – 'Reach is another key marker we have to look out for, but it isn't always an indicator of whether or not an audience will engage positively with branded content.'

OP TALENT

OP Talent was founded in 2012 by former tech industry mogul Liam Chivers. He saw the potential of vlogging ahead of the crowd and quit his successful job to manage vloggers. Olajide 'KSI' Olatunji was one of his first signings. At the time, KSI had just 100,000 subscribers. But Chivers' gamble paid off as KSI grew his audience and now has 15 million subscribers across both his channels and 130 million video views a month. Chivers and his team make deals worth five- and six-figure sums with brands looking to expand their audience.

OP Talent specialises in managing vloggers who cover video-gaming – OP is video-game speak for 'overpowered', which means that a character or group in the game has become too powerful. OP Talent's roster of clients is super-strong, notching up a mind-blowing 40 million subscribers between them.

In January 2016, OP Talent was sold to global media enterprise Endemol Shine. That such a massive media company took notice of a YouTube talent agency managing independent gaming vloggers shows just how seriously traditional media is taking 'new' media. As a result of the deal, Endemol Shine has announced plans to push the OP Talent clients to international audiences and give them more TV-deal opportunities.

OP Talent's roster: KSI, Ali-A, ComedyShorts Gamer, Harry Lewis (W2S).

OP Talent's brand deals: OP Talent has matched KSI with Microsoft Xbox One, Mad Catz, BT Sport and Orion publishers for a book entitled *KSI: I Am a Bellend*; Ali-A with KontrolFreek and Scuf Gaming; and ComedyShortsGamer with UT Coin Traders.

OP Talent founder Liam Chivers' advice: Engage with subscribers – 'KSI is really good at speaking to fans – he really tries to engage with everyone on his channel and he once thanked every person who tweeted about buying one of his music tracks – probably near 1,000 individual mentions. This makes his followers really feel like they're involved,' Chivers told CNN.

Be yourself – 'KSI is very personable and the fans feel they can relate to him,' Chivers added in the same CNN interview. 'KSI played the UK's biggest game but what set him apart was his content, and that's what got people heavily into – his content is so much more than videos about FIFA.'

ADDITION LLC

Addition was set up in 2013 by Petar Mandich and two former colleagues from the Collective, a YouTube multi-channel network. One of Petar's first signings was Justine Ezarik, who is known as iJustine to her 2.7 million subscribers. 'We just hit it off,' Mandich explained to *LA Weekly*. 'We had a good understanding of her brand, and what she needs to build her business.'

Justine recommended Mandich to other vloggers, which resulted in the signing of clients like Cat 'Catrific' Valdes and Joey Graceffa. Joey makes no secret that he is hugely influenced by iJustine in his memoir *In Real Life: My Journey to a Pixelated World*. He remembers how he was just one of her many fans at first. She started to notice him when his videos gained more traffic and they began to interact. Therefore when he grew to need a manager, he asked Justine and she recommended Addition.

Addition's talent roster: iJustine, Joey Graceffa, Cat Valdes, Dulce Candy.

Addition's brand deals: Addition has matched iJustine with AT&T, Canon and Walgreens; Joey Graceffa with H&R Block and Simon & Schuster; and Dulce Candy with Crest 3D White, L'Oréal, Olay and Macy's.

Addition Head of Talent Petar Mandich's advice: Be entrepreneurial – 'I admire each one of our creators for taking the chance, investing in themselves and for essentially becoming their own boss,'Mandich told *Entrepreneur Magazine*. 'It shows audiences who maybe don't know what they want to do with their lives that they can do something entrepreneurial, too.'

Be open – 'Joey Graceffa recently came out, and he wanted to create some content to share his story and empower his audience and fans who might be struggling with identity and confusion. It was very well received,' Mandich revealed to *LA Weekly*.

Q & A: CASSEY HO

Cassey Ho from the YouTube channel Blogilates is on Mode Media's talent roster. She explained how she built her following and how long it took, in an interview with *EContent magazine*. Her journey is very inspiring.

Q: How long did it take you to build a following?

CASSEY: I posted my first video in October 2009, and here I am today with over 2.8 million subscribers on both my YouTube channels. I am fortunate and so grateful for each and every one of my POPsters.

Q: What do you think sets your vlog apart?

CASSEY: I think I have seen so much growth because I am transparent, and am not afraid to be super-happy on or off YouTube. Personally, I train better when I am being encouraged, so I am not as aggressive or stern as many trainers, and my fans really seem to like it that way! I also keep my videos fun and playful so that my POPsters look forward to exercising because it's like we're just hanging out together.

Q: What advice would you give someone who has an idea for a vlog but is afraid to get started?

CASSEY: I would say go for it! It can take a while to build a strong and consistent fan base, so don't expect to launch and have 100,000 likes in a day. Also, *do not focus on the numbers*. Focus on doing what you do best. It's about building a community of people who want to visit the site every day because you create value and offer expertise. If you don't try, you will never know what might have been!

What are you waiting for? Get online and find out more about each company. Also, enter 'YouTube talent agency' and 'social talent agency' into Google to find details of smaller and newer agencies. Once you're signed up to an agency, someone else will be helping you make money – and that someone else is likely to be an expert with years of experience in doing deals with brands. This could lead to opportunities you may never have discovered on your own, and more money as a result.

Working with Talent Managers

After reading this chapter, you should have:

☐ Researched Gleam Futures, Mode Media, OP Talent and Addition LLP
☐ Taken notice of the advice given by the founders of these companies
☐ Used Google to search for smaller and newer talent agencies

CHAPTER 11

HOW TO EARN EXTRA REVENUE BY BLOGGING

Successful vloggers have multiple revenue streams and YouTube is only one of them. To make serious money from vlogging, you need to build up your brand beyond YouTube and look at ways to market and sell your content both online and offline. This chapter looks at ways to expand your brand online, and we'll explore offline content like merchandise and product lines in the next chapter.

All of the vloggers on *Forbes* magazine's 2015 list of the top ten richest vloggers have a blog in addition to their YouTube channels. As it's always a good idea to research what successful people are doing, so you can copy the best bits and add your own unique twist, you should have a look at the blogs made by these vloggers:

- PewDiePie (estimated wealth £12 million) – www.pewdiepie.com
- Smosh by Ian Hecox and Anthony Padilla (estimated wealth £8.5 million) – www.smosh.com
- Fine Brothers by Benny and Rafi Fine (estimated wealth £8.5 million) – www.thefinebros.tumblr.com/
- Lindsey Stirling (estimated wealth £6 million) – www.LindseyStirling.com
- Rhett and Link (estimated wealth £4.5 million) – www.rhettandlink.com
- KSI (estimated wealth £4.5 million) – www.ksiolajidebt.com/
- Michelle Phan (estimated wealth £3 million) – MichellePhan.com
- Superwoman by Lilly Singh (estimated wealth £2.5 million) –
- http://lillysingh.blogspot.co.uk/
- Roman Atwood (estimated wealth £2.5 million) – http://romanatwood.com/
- Rosanna Pansino (estimated wealth £2.5 million) – http://rosannapansino.com/
- Zoella (wealth unknown) – www.zoella.co.uk
- Jim Chapman (estimated wealth £1.5 million) – www.jimchapman.co.uk
- Tanya Burr (estimated wealth (£1.5 million) – www.tanyaburr.co.uk
- Sprinkle of Glitter (wealth unknown) – sprinkleofglitter.blogspot.com
- Charlieissocoollike (wealth unknown) – http://charliemcdonnell.com/

Making a blog and writing posts takes time, but the financial incentive is high. Once you have a blog you can make money through Google AdSense, affiliate marketing, direct advertising, sponsored reviews and branded merchandise. That's on top of the money you'll earn through YouTube advertising revenue and making sponsored videos for brands.

So how do you create a successful blog? I have written a whole book on this subject (called *Get Rich Blogging*). That book takes readers from the concept of a blog, to thinking about branding and image, to turning followers into money. As we have already considered branding and image in this book, let me sum up the practical side of setting up a blog and the ways to monetise it.

BUILDING AND MAINTAINING A BLOG

Have you heard of WordPress (wordpress.com) or Blogger (blogger.com)? These websites allow you to host a blog on their platforms for free. However, I don't recommend creating one of these free accounts as they aren't enabled for adverts. This means you'll struggle to monetise a blog hosted on the free WordPress or Blogger platforms.

As the goal of this chapter – and the book – is to explore ways of making money, I advise you to set up your own website to host your blog. This is known as self-hosting. If you've started a free blog previously, you can copy and paste all your old content into your new self-hosted blog.

Self-hosting involves buying a domain name and a web-hosting account, and then installing a blogging service that enables you to write posts. This sounds complicated but when you break it down into simple steps it's so easy that most vloggers have no trouble doing it themselves without hiring an expensive web-designer. These are the steps you need to take:

Step one: Visit a hosting company's website. I recommend GoDaddy (uk.godaddy.com) or Bluehost (bluehost.com).

Step two: Click *Get Started* and follow the steps until you see a box where you can enter a domain name. Check that your domain name is available. In an ideal world, your domain name should be the same name as your vlog. However, try your name or your full name including middle name if that's not available. You could also use your name with 'vlogger' or 'vlogs' on the end.

Step three: Once you've found your domain name, select your hosting plan. Start with the most basic package. There is no point spending a lot of money on a package before you've even written one blog post. You might find that you don't like blogging after a few weeks, and then you'll have wasted your money. When you started making videos, you started with a basic camera, lighting and editing kit, and then upgraded it when you knew you enjoyed it and you were attracting followers. The same is true for blogging – start with the basics and upgrade when you get more traffic.

Step four: Don't buy any additional extras. GoDaddy might ask if you want a package that installs and maintains WordPress for you. This is not necessary because WordPress is simple to install, so you'll be spending money on something you can easily do yourself. In addition to this, you will have to go through GoDaddy every time you want to make changes to your WordPress account, and this is time-consuming. You'll have a lot more control over your blog if you install WordPress yourself.

Step five: Once you've bought your domain, you should receive a confirmation email with your login name and password. Log in to your account. If you're using BlueHost, you'll see a cPanel. Navigate to the Mojo Marketplace section and click on the *One Click Installs* icon. Choose *WordPress* and follow the steps to set up your WordPress account.

If using GoDaddy, navigate to the Popular Apps section and click *WordPress*. Click *Install Now* and follow the steps to set up your account.

When your account is set up you'll receive an email explaining how to log in to your WordPress dashboard. It's usually your domain name with /wp-admin at the end, for example 'yourdomain.com/wp-admin'.

Log in to your WordPress account and play around. The first screen you'll see is the dashboard. From there you can follow the links in the sidebar to add posts and pages. You'll be using the Add Posts function most often, so click on that and explore how to use it. You'll see a large box in the centre of the screen where you write your content. Above that there are little buttons to format the text such as font size, boldness and colour of the text, and add links. At the right-hand side of the screen, there is a box that allows you to choose when you want your post to be published – you can either post it live straight away or schedule it for a later date. You can also create categories that help you to organise the design of your blog. When you've created a lot of posts, your readers will appreciate being able to navigate quickly to the category they're most interested in.

BLOG DESIGN AND CONTENT

You can see what your blog looks like by removing '/wp-admin' from the URL. The first time you do this you may be a bit shocked by how basic it looks. Don't worry, because it's simple to change. You don't need any technical knowledge. All you need is your vlog logo, an idea of the colours and features you want to have on your blog and the website ThemeForest (themeforest.net).

By features, I mean functions like a slider to display your latest blog posts, a timer to count down to an important date or a video-player that automatically displays your most recent vlog. To get an idea of what's possible, check out the list of blogs at the start of this chapter. Note down features you like so you can pick a theme from ThemeForest that includes those things.

It's very important to take time over the design of your blog. Not only does it reflect your brand, but it determines how long people will spend on your blog. Nobody wants to spend time trawling through a chaotic, disorganised jumble, so you need to make your blog as easy to read as possible to attract traffic that you can monetise. How? When designing your blog, have the phrase 'ARE CAPTAINS' in mind. Each letter stands for a design element that you must have on your blog. When you get your blog design right, you can sail off and captain your blog to find the treasure waiting in the blogosphere. And by 'treasure' I mean money, which you will earn if you get the design right.

ARE CAPTAINS

A – Attractive 'wow' elements: For example, I use stars in the Live Like a VIP header instead of block page dividers. Since the design is different, it stands out.

R – Readable: It's vital to make sure people can go to your site, get the information they want and leave quickly. Check there are no fancy design elements getting in the way of how easy it is to read and navigate the site. It's all very well having a pretty pastel font, but if people can't read it, it will be a hindrance to traffic.

E – Easy to brand: You need to keep getting your logo in people's faces so they start to remember you. If you brand t-shirts and posters to drive traffic, then you need the same image online to make sure people realise they are in the right place. The more someone sees an image, the more it will stick in their head.

C – Comments space: By now, you should be getting some comments underneath your videos when you upload them to YouTube. If you plan to embed your videos into your blog posts, then it's a good idea to install some comment facility when you design your blog so that viewers can comment directly underneath relevant posts without having to go to YouTube. The longer people spend on your blog, the better!

A – Advert space: If there is no space for adverts in the sidebar, you will never be able to make money from your blog. It sounds obvious, but so many bloggers overlook this when trying to fill up their blog with special features.

P – Picture sizes: If you are going to have pictures in the main section of your blog, how big should they be? This depends on what size you've designed the main section of your blog. The size of your sidebar is also important if you're planning on having some banner ads. Most ads can be up to 300 pixels wide, so you need to make sure you have sufficient room.

T – Tone: The tone of the colour used in the design will influence how people react to your site. Pinks get us in the mood for a girly gossip, while a black-and-white site is more suitable to a businesslike news blog. Above all, your blog colours should be the same as the colours you used for your YouTube channel design and logo.

A – 'About us' section: Firstly, you want to make sure that people who find you through the blog know you have a YouTube channel. Secondly, you want potential advertisers to contact you about possible deals, so it is vital you have a space explaining how fabulous you are as well as how they can contact you.

I – Information search box: As blogs display the most recent information at the top, it can be hard to find articles that were written a few weeks ago. Most bloggers like to make life easier for their readers by installing a search box so they can easily locate an article on a specific subject (I have one at Live Like a VIP in the top right). Leave room for this search box somewhere in the design of your site.

N – Names of other bloggers you rate: In other words, a blog-roll. This is brilliant for search engine optimisation, so you need to design your blog with it in mind.

S – Statistics monitoring tool: Make sure you sign up for an account with Google Analytics (google.com/analytics) and install its code so you can monitor your blog's traffic, in the same way that you use YouTube Analytics to monitor how much vlog traffic you get and how long people watch your videos. Statistics are vital, as advertisers like to know facts and figures when you're ready to monetise the blog.

With your design wishlist firmly in mind, visit ThemeForest. On this site, you'll see thousands of readymade WordPress designs that you can customise with your logo and content. Each theme costs between £20 and £50. Don't go for a complicated design, as you won't be updating your blog enough to fill out all the sections. After all, the blog is secondary to your vlog and you'll be spending more time creating awesome videos than you will be writing blog posts. Keep things simple by choosing an elegant design with a white background. You will be able to customise the header area by inserting your logo and alter the design further using your colours and fonts. Customisation is relatively simple to do. Once you have purchased a theme you'll receive an instruction manual along with the theme design. The theme design files and instruction manual come in one large zip file that you download to your desktop. I advise opening the zip file and dragging the instructions file to your desktop so you can consult it regularly.

You should then drag the other folder (i.e. the one that doesn't contain the instruction manual) to your desktop so you can upload it to WordPress and start using it. Navigate to the dashboard of your WordPress account. In the left sidebar you'll see *Appearance* and when you hover your mouse over it you'll see *Themes*. Click *Themes* then *Add New*. Upload the folder from your desktop, click *Install* and it's all done. To check that it's worked, remove /wp-admin from the Wordpress URL and you should see the design has changed dramatically from the first time you looked at it.

Follow the instructions in the manual to customise the header, colours and any other design elements you wish. As soon as you do this it will look better, but it won't feel like yours until you add some content.

CONTENT

Content is king, for bloggers as well as vloggers. Therefore you need to give people content they can't access anywhere else. This means you can't simply embed your videos into blog posts without giving readers anything else. If your videos are already on YouTube, there's no extra incentive for people to visit your blog.

Start by explaining videos in blog posts to give your viewers and readers that little bit more. Every time you make a video, create a blog post related to it using photos and text summing up the video's subject. If you interviewed someone in the video, you could provide a transcript of the interview on your blog, and leave a bit out so people have to watch the video to find out everything. If you've done a beauty tutorial, take before-and-after pics, tell the readers about the products you used and refer them to the video to watch everything.

Once you're confident creating this type of content, you could write some blogs about the process of video creation. Give people behind-the-scenes access on a vlog shoot – for example, outtakes, showing footage or stills of scenes you messed up. Write about how vlogging makes you feel, and explain why you enjoy doing it and what your goals are. The more personal you can be in your blog posts the better, as you're aiming to be a friend to all your blog readers just as you are to all your vlog viewers.

WordPress enables you to embed video, and I recommend doing this at the end of each blog post that refers to a particular vlog. This is because the blog post should have intrigued people enough to make them watch the video, and you don't want a reader to navigate away from your site. If you embed the videos in your blog posts, you'll still notch up the video views on YouTube, but you'll be keeping people on your blog for longer. This is important because when you're chatting to potential advertisers for your blog, they will ask about the average amount of time your audience spends on it. To embed a vlog, navigate to the YouTube video you want to copy, click on the *Share* button underneath the *Subscribe* button, and then click on the *Embed* tab. Copy and paste the code into a blog post when the *Text* tab at the top right of the writing area is enabled (as opposed to the *Html* tab).

I update my blog Live Like a VIP at least once a day; and when I interviewed successful bloggers for my book *Get Rich Blogging*, I found they did the same. Because the primary goal of most people reading this book is to 'get rich vlogging', it's not necessary to update this often as you'll be spending more time on your vlogs. Could you aim for one update every other day? You'll find that blogging is a lot less time-consuming than vlogging. If you only have time to create a single video a week, it's hard to make people engage with you as you're only in their lives for three to four minutes a week. But if you can create three or four blog posts that week, then you're showing off more of your personality, keeping people entertained and making them eagerly anticipate your next vlog. Whether the blog posts consist of behind-the-scenes pictures and content, short how-to articles, teasers, tips, updates or news about what's happening in your niche (such as new make-up products or computer games), it all helps to keep your viewers' attention.

Be prepared to make vlogs based on reactions to your blog, or blog posts based on comments to videos you've made. If a particular blog post is well-received, with a lot of comments and shares on social media, then you should thank people for their comments and show you've read them. You can do this with a follow-up video, which will further encourage your blog readers to check out your YouTube channel. Conversely, if you've received some useful or strange comments underneath a YouTube video, tell your blog readers about it and this will encourage blog readers to check out your channel.

TIP: BE SPECIFIC!

The key to creating great content is the same whether you're vlogging or blogging – you have to specialise. There are more than 152 million blogs on the Internet and most of those blogs get fewer than 1,000 visitors a month, which will barely bring in enough revenue to cover web-hosting costs. The reason these blogs are struggling is because there are no key factors that make them stand out from other blogs. Many beauty blogs tend to copy other beauty blogs without adding extra elements, and many fashion and tech blogs are guilty of the same crime.

To be the best in a certain field, you need to narrow the

pitch. It's hard to be the best beauty blogger/vlogger or the best fitness blogger/vlogger when you're competing with people who started blogging/vlogging years ago and have grown a loyal audience over time. However, there may be a certain niche that the others don't address in as much detail as you are able to provide. For example, say you want to cover fitness. Work out what part of fitness you enjoy the most. Is it following a specific diet like Atkins or the 5:2 Diet? Or is it attending a specific exercise class like CrossFit or weightlifting? Now work out what age range and sex you want to appeal to. Is it young women in their twenties who want to weightlift or is it middle-aged men who want to diet? You can narrow it down even further by combining diet and exercise, such as weightlifting for vegetarian women in their twenties, or middle-aged men on Atkins starting to run long distances.

Once you own that particular topic and you are seen as the go-to source for information on that topic, you can start to branch out. But it's important to establish yourself as an expert first, because that's what makes other bloggers/vloggers want to collaborate with you. When you're the expert in your field, others feel like they have something to gain by collaborating. You may not be able to offer them traffic at the start, but you can offer them specialised expertise. Once you've collaborated, others have linked to you and your traffic's growing, then it's time to test out a wider range of subjects on your audience.

MONETISING A BLOG

You can monetise a blog in the following ways:

Google AdSense Google's AdSense programme is a highly-specific advertising placement service made by Google. It uses keyword targeting and other factors to place ads on your blog and/or YouTube channel that will be of interest to your viewers and readers. The blog ads are either text- or image-based, and they are specifically targeted at people who enjoy the kind of content that you provide. When someone visits your blog and clicks on an advertisement, you earn a commission from Google for providing the space for that advertisement.

The more people who engage with these ads on your blog, the more you earn. However, make sure never to encourage clicks or engagement with these advertisements in any sort of way, as this is against the AdSense terms of service and it will get your account flagged or banned.

To use Google AdSense on your blog, follow the steps below.

Visit the Google AdSense homepage (google.com/Adsense) and click on the *Sign-up* button in the upper right-hand corner of the screen.

Fill in the online application form, which will ask for the URL of your blog, its primary language and confirmation that you agree to the terms and conditions of the Google AdSense programme. It will also ask you for your bank details so you can receive payments.

Have a detailed look at what type of advertising is available to you. You have the option of image-based ads and text-based ads, and you can pick the size of your adverts. When you see a type of advert that you'd like to use, the process is not that much more complicated than embedding a YouTube video into your blog. Google Ads will display an html code next to the ad you've selected, and you can copy and paste this code into a blog post.

Alternatively, you could place an AdSense advert in the sidebar of your blog, rather than in an individual blog post. To do this, go to your WordPress dashboard and click *Appearances* in the left menu bar. This will bring up a drop-down menu, from which you should select *Widgets*. Once in the Widgets menu, you will see a large table containing rectangular boxes. Can you see one that says '*text*'? You'll need that later. To the right of the menu you will see a list of boxes labelling different areas of your blog such as header, right sidebar, left sidebar etc. If you want the advert in your left sidebar, click on the relevant box and it will expand. Now go back to the main table, and click and hold your mouse on the box that says '*text*'. Drag it into the left sidebar box. Once you let go of the mouse, the text box will stay in the left sidebar area.

Click on the text box itself and it will expand.

Paste the html code into the text box and hit *Save*. Adverts will now appear in the sidebar.

TIP: WATCH THE ADSENSE TUTORIAL VIDEO

If you want to see a step-by-step video demonstration of how to install Google AdSense on your blog, go to Google and search for 'AdSense installation video'. A video tutorial shows you exactly what to do and where to click, and you can pause it as you work through the installation process.

AFFILIATE MARKETING

Affiliate marketing involves taking a commission by referring a customer to a product. For example, if I write a blog post about a song by a new artist and link to where my readers can buy the track on Amazon, I will receive money every time one of my readers buys it. Through what's known as a cookie, the retailer is able to track where the customer came from and realise it was my blog that referred them to the sale. There are lots of affiliate programmes available; you can do deals with individual retailers like Argos or Amazon, or many different companies at once by signing up to affiliate networks.

If you get it right, affiliate marketing can be a lucrative way to make money, especially if you get high levels of traffic. Bloggers can earn as much as 8 to 10 per cent of a sale through affiliate revenue. However, this doesn't mean you should make every link an affiliate link. It's tempting to do so because the more links you include in your posts, the more chance you have of making money. However, if you recommend products too often or plug items your readers don't need, you could lose traffic as your readers start to feel like you're cashing in rather than giving them useful advice or information. Readers who feel like they're being used will be put off your blog.

When starting out, most bloggers prefer to join a network of affiliates rather than set up accounts with lots of individual retailers. You could deal directly with large retailers like Argos or Amazon, but you will receive your commission in fits and starts and you'll have to deal with correspondence from each individual affiliate. If you join a network that has several brands on its books, then you earn whenever you promote one of these brands, giving you more potential income – plus you will receive payment from one central source. Larger affiliate network agencies also allow you to choose banner adverts for your blog, which you can display in your blog's sidebar or below the header. When someone clicks on the banner, they'll be taken to the advertiser's site and you'll receive commission if that person buys something.

To join an affiliate network, simply visit their website (listed below), sign up to create an account and you're away. Each time you log in to your account on that network, you'll see which brands you can link to and how much commission you make from each brand. Then you can decide whether to link to brands inside your posts, use their banner ads or both.

Signing up for an account with one affiliate network does not preclude you from joining another, but do remember more schemes mean more stress as you'll need to monitor your earnings from all the different places.

Some popular affiliate networks are Affiliate Window (uk. affiliatewindow.com), LinkShare (linkshare.co.uk), and Affiliate Future (affiliatefuture.co.uk). Have a look at their websites and see what suits you best!

TIP: USE SKIMLINKS

Skimlinks (skimlinks.com) is the UK's fastest-growing affiliate provider as it gives its members access to all the affiliate networks. It's simple to use from the moment you sign up, as a Skimlinks account automatically means you'll be able to earn money from all the brands on the database. There is no need to sign up to each affiliate individually.

Every time you're thinking of recommending a product in a blog post, check to see if the product retailer is in the Skimlinks scheme. If so, link to them in the normal way and you'll receive a commission. Again, be careful with how you use Skimlinks so you don't annoy your readers. While it might be tempting to browse Skimlinks' list of retailers and then tailor a blog post to guarantee you can link to some of them, you need to make sure your blog post contains useful and interesting information on the same subject you usually cover. Otherwise your readers will be able to tell that you're only writing to make sales, which will make them feel used and less inclined to read your blog in future.

Pay attention to Skimlinks' monthly reports. Not only do these make it really easy for you to keep track of earnings, but you can also monitor what schemes are working for you and what your readers aren't interested in. The monthly reports contain statistics on the most-clicked links on your blog, how many times they were clicked and how much you earned from those clicks.

DIRECT ADVERTISING

As blogging has become more popular, businesses and brands are allocating more of their advertising budgets to online activity. This means we're seeing a rise in the number of specialist online-based advertising agencies. The ad agency staff makes deals with large companies and distributes the ads among the bloggers they have on their books.

Given the choice, most bloggers would rather use an agency than Google AdSense as there's more human interaction and control. With Google AdSense there is always a risk of an unsuitable advert popping up on your blog, as Google's content-matching algorithm can be temperamental at times. Also, ad agencies have more transparent pricing structures. Google never makes it clear what percentage of commission it takes for selling your ads, but agencies tend to split revenue 50:50 and give you a contract at the start, laying out terms and conditions. In most cases you are guaranteed to get paid, as you'll receive money for hosting an ad on your site for a specific period of time or for writing a favourable product review. In contrast, Google AdSense only pays you if people click on the ads.

Not all bloggers are able to sign up with an ad agency at the start of their blogging journeys, as agencies have specific criteria about whom they take on. Ad agencies are staffed by real people and these people need to be paid. If an agency doesn't believe it can match your advertising space to any of its regular clients, then it won't welcome you as you won't generate them any revenue.

The only way you'll find out if you qualify is to ask. Investigate the websites of Handpicked (handpickedmedia.co.uk) or Mode Media (corp.mode.com) to see how to submit your blog. If they turn you down, then you've still got Google AdSense making you money.

You could also try selling your own adverts. This will be more successful the better known you are in your niche and the more specialised you are, as advertisers like to know that they are reaching a specific target audience. It is a lot of work, and you are solely responsible for keeping the brands happy because you can't delegate to an advertising agency. However, you won't have to share the commission, so there's potential to make more money.

TIP: EMAIL POTENTIAL ADVERTISERS

Selling adverts requires great organisational skills and a lot of persistence. Start by making a list of brands you know, and then add brands that have worked with other bloggers in your niche. Finally, add brands that have the same target audience as your blog.

Find out direct email addresses for people in marketing departments at those brands. If these are unavailable or hard to find online, call customer services. A generic email always gets ignored so there's no point in sending it. Write down a personal email address next to every brand on your list.

Create an email outlining that advertising opportunities are available and giving some statistics for your site. Don't give them prices just yet as you want to test interest and tempt them into replying to you, at which point you can negotiate a deal.

Don't be put off if few brands reply. Chase them up a couple of days later with phone calls, and work down the list until every brand is ticked off. There are hundreds of reasons why a brand might not have replied, which have nothing to do with whether or not it will advertise. The email might have found its way to your contact's spam folder, they might be unwell or on holiday, or they might be powerless to answer your query as it's the role of someone in a different department. Find out what's behind the

---

lack of reply, and solve the problem by emailing someone else or by listening to the reasons why they're reluctant to advertise and coming up with solutions. You may find that they were just taking time to look at their budget, and were just about to email you back and say yes. In that case – negotiate your deal! Your price should take into account the size of the brand as bigger companies expect to spend more on advertising. It should also reflect the amount of traffic your blog gets and the amount of time it will take you to do any additional work for the brand like sponsored posts or advertorials.

For more detail on how to sell blog advertising, see my book *Get Rich Blogging*.

ADVERTORIALS AND SPONSORED POSTS

An advertorial is when an advert is designed to look like editorial content on your blog. This essentially means an advertiser will ask you to write a post about a certain subject and recommend a specific product, and you'll be paid when you publish it.

Some bloggers view getting paid to post as a dirty business, but if you have tried out the product and believe it works, what have you got to lose by writing a blog post and earning money from it? If a PR agency sends me a sample of a new shampoo and I like it, then I'd probably recommend it. So why is it different when an advertiser sends me a sample of a product and tells me I'll earn money if I review it?

At the start of your blogging career, advertorials are a fantastic way to earn income as they typically earn bloggers £50-£100 per post. In month one of your blog you won't be earning that much from Google AdSense or affiliate networks.

If you'd like to start getting advertorials, sign up to an agency like Teads (teads.tv/en/) or PayPerPost (payperpost.com) and they'll send you a brief. Follow their instructions, submit the post URL and you can expect payment within thirty days.

Alternatively, you can approach a brand directly. Reach out to the companies that make products you'd like to review for your viewers and readers, and see what they're willing to do for you.

Some companies will only go as far as to provide free products, which is useful if these are products you like to use anyway. Other companies will partner with you and sponsor your post or blog in exchange for a detailed, high-quality review of one of their products. Don't be dismayed if you only get brands offering free products at the start, as free products could lead to sponsorship later down the line. For example, you might write a blog post about a make-up brand which your readers find really useful so they comment on and share it. You would show this interaction to the product manufacturer and they'd see that you have influence and want to work with you in the future. Next time they approached you with an offer of free products, you could point out how much traffic the last post got and say that you expect a fee for your review this time.

BRANDED MERCHANDISE

Creating branded merchandise and clothing for your blog has never been easier. Print-on-demand sites like CaféPress, Zazzle and Spreadshirt let you upload your own designs to create branded merchandise including t-shirts, posters, mugs and mobile-phone cases to sell online.

Print-on-demand services are completely free to use, so you won't need to raise any start-up funds to make your merchandise. All you have to do is register, upload your designs, choose what products to put your designs on (from t-shirts to bags to cameras) and then create an online store. Often, you will receive a short piece of code to embed into your blog so that you can host the online store on your site too. You will also get code for ad banners and blog widgets that can direct your blog readers to your online store.

Another benefit is that there are no administration costs. You don't have to pay for shipping, nor do you have to spend time queuing up at the Post Office. You don't even have to work out how many products to make in advance. This is because these print-on-demand sites make up your orders as they come in and ship them off for you, deducting the costs from your profit. All you have to do is pick the design and everything else is taken care of – from the manufacturing to the shipping to customer services in case of returns or complaints.

TIP: CONSULT YOUR AUDIENCE AS YOU DESIGN MERCHANDISE
Make your blog readers and vlog viewers feel involved with the creation of the merchandise by consulting them during the design process. Write a blog post showing people different design ideas, and create a vlog about what you're doing and why. Ask viewers to send in suggestions. If your audience is involved in the design process, they're more likely to buy the finished product. Plus it reminds your audience that you

value their opinion, and when people feel valued, they stay loyal to a brand.

More information on all of these monetisation methods can be found in my book *Get Rich Blogging*.

Here are some case studies of successful bloggers, looking at how they started their blogs and grew traffic from scratch:

FASHION BLOGGER CASE STUDY: THE CLOTHES WHISPERER

Kristin Knox from The Clothes Whisperer (theclothes whisperer.co.uk) has written two books– *Alexander McQueen: Genius of a Generation* and *Culture to Catwalk: How World Cultures Influence Fashion*. The Clothes Whisperer has over 10,000 Facebook fans.

Q: What advice would you give to an aspiring fashion blogger?

Kristin: Stay true to yourself, as cheesy as it sounds. Don't try to position yourself against the 'superbloggers' or sites like WWD, Style.com or other fashion authorities. Leave the expertise to the experts; bring your own experience to the table and find a unique way of talking about fashion, be it fashion and food, fashion and babies, fashion and yoga...whatever!

Q: What's a typical daily routine for a fashion blogger?

Kristin: There is no such thing as a 'typical' day, which is why I feel blessed to do what I do. I guess the quotidian consistencies would include checking of email, checking of Twitter, scheduling of posts (once to twice a week) and charging of lots of various electronics. Other than that, just

---

doing what journalists do: that is to say, going out, meeting people, seeing things and experiencing fashion life.

Q: How can a blogger spread the word?

Kristin: I guess being mentioned in the press helped. I just grew steadily. I'd rather have quality readers over quantity.

BEAUTY BLOGGER CASE STUDY: BRITISH BEAUTY BLOGGER

Jane Cunningham from British Beauty Blogger has had a column in *The Guardian* and regularly writes for the *Huffington Post* blog. She has written beauty books – *The Compact Book of Being Beautiful* and *101 Beauty Tips: The Modern Woman's Guide to Looking Good and Feeling Great*. Jane has over 18,000 Twitter followers.

Q: If a blogger is starting from nowhere, how can they build up their followers?

Jane: The best advice I can give is to follow other bloggers and start a relationship with them. Comment on their posts and follow them on Facebook and Twitter. This will get you noticed by their followers and, hopefully, traffic will rise on your site. Comment, comment, comment! Basically, just shout the loudest.

Q: How do you engage the readers through Twitter and Facebook and maintain a conversation?

Jane: I get more tweets than I can possibly answer. But I do really try and get back to everyone, even if it is only briefly, as it is important that readers think we are a community.

Q: How can bloggers use Twitter and Facebook to get web traffic up?

Jane: The more you interact with readers on Twitter, the more others pick up on it. I have also introduced giveaways on my page, which have increased my traffic by 31 per cent, massive when you think of it in thousands.

Q: How often should a beauty blogger update?

Jane: At least three times a week if you want to grow a community.

Q: How long did it take you to make money from your blog?

Jane: It has been a slow process. Blogging is still my second job as I work in fashion retail head office, which is my main income. I am making money out of the blog now, but that is due to advertisers. I have also given some talks at colleges in Manchester as a beauty expert, which I get paid for.

After reading through this chapter, you should have:

☐ Looked at some of the blogs made by successful vloggers

☐ Bought a domain name and basic hosting package

☐ Installed WordPress

☐ Used ThemeForest to change the design of a generic WordPress blog

☐ Registered for and installed Google AdSense

☐ Joined some affiliate networks

☐ Contacted brands to ask for money or products in exchange for posts

☐ Looked at print-on-demand merchandising websites like Zazzle and CaféPress

CHAPTER 12

CREATING YOUR OWN PRODUCT LINE, BOOK AND MUSIC

Once you've built a loyal audience who regularly watch your vlogs and buy brands' products when you recommend them, the next step is to create your own product lines. You'll make a profit every time someone buys one of your products, which usually ends up being significantly more than the fee you receive from a brand for plugging their collections.

For example, beauty vlogger Michelle Phan has done huge deals with world-famous brands like Dr Pepper and Lancôme. However, the real money is coming in from her own beauty e-commerce business Ipsy. This is a beauty-box subscription service, where users pay a monthly fee of ten dollars in exchange for monthly boxes of sample-sized beauty products. Promoting Ipsy to her 8 million YouTube subscribers has led to 700,000 people taking out monthly subscriptions, and Ipsy has an annual turnover of $84 million. Business analysts value the company as being worth $500 million.

In the UK, Sam and Nicki Chapman from the vlog Pixiwoo were among the first to earn money with their own product range. Helped by Dominic Smales from Gleam Futures, the girls launched a line of make-up brushes called Real Techniques in 2011. By 2014, it was the best-selling make-up brush brand in the UK, beating MAC. 'It's real and genuine and 100 per cent relatable,' Sam Chapman told *Glamour* when asked why some vloggers had received so much success over the past ten years. 'There is usually something to promote or sell in a magazine, but vlogging isn't like that. People now recognise us in the street, but only people who watch our vlog. Despite our following [nearly 2 million YouTube subscribers], not everyone knows who we are. It's only people who watch and like us that know who we are, so we never get any negative comments in the street. How fantastic is that?'

Zoe Sugg is also cashing in from product lines. She teamed up with Superdrug in 2014 to make her own range of beauty products like body spray and bubblebath. When they first went on sale, dedicated fans stayed up until midnight to be the first to purchase the products. The Superdrug website received twice as much traffic as usual, but that accounted for only 75 per cent of sales as 25 per cent of customers bought products from Zoe's own website. Several of Superdrug's 800 stores sold out of products on the first day, and Superdrug say one product was sold every two seconds during the first twenty-four hours. This makes it one of Superdrug's best-ever celebrity lines, and a second collection was released in summer 2015 containing more product lines. Simon Comins, Buying Director at Superdrug, said: 'We have been amazed at how successful Zoella's collections have been, and this latest range has really superseded sales expectations. Zoe has created some truly amazing products for our customers that are literally flying off the shelves. Zoella really resonates with our shoppers; she has an epic fan base that is as passionate about products as she is.'

Zoe's friend Tanya Burr became a make-up entrepreneur in 2014, when she launched her own range of lip glosses and nail varnish. At the start it was sold exclusively on the beauty website Feel Unique (feelunique.com), and pre-orders for the range amassed the largest waiting-list Feel Unique has ever had. They sold so well that she developed more products and now has a collection of thirty-one eye palettes, lipsticks, glosses and blushers, which are sold at Superdrug and Feel Unique. She wants the range to grow even further, then plans to sit back and enjoy the money coming in. 'I would love my own make-up counter because that's where I started,' she told *Glamour,* referring to her days working at a beauty counter for the make-up brand Laura Mercier. 'I'd be going full circle. Then I could go and work on it one day a week.'

Other vloggers-turned-product-entrepreneurs include Ruth Crilly from the vlog A Model Recommends, who has a best-selling dry-shampoo range at Superdrug and Feel Unique and Fleur Bell, who runs the vlog Fleur De Force and has a range of eyelashes produced by Eyelure. Samantha Maria, a.k.a. Beauty Crush, has her own clothing collection at Novem & Knight (novemknight.com).

Anyone can come up with a product range – once you've worked out what would fit with the theme of your vlog – but getting it stocked in stores such as Superdrug is not so easy. Established stores are unwilling to take risks on vloggers until they can guarantee their products will sell. The viewing figures of vloggers like Tanya Burr and Zoella speak for themselves; however, don't feel you have to wait until you have millions of followers to develop a product. If you have a passion for it, then that's half the battle, as motivation will help you break down barriers on the path to getting it manufactured and stocked in stores.

Ask yourself if you truly believe your vlog's audience would buy the products that you're thinking of. If the answer is yes, then you can produce and make them yourself. Once you've proved people are buying the product you're making, it's easier to convince stores to stock it. After all, they'll want a piece of the profits.

Perhaps the easiest way to start is by selling merchandise related to your vlog. Multi-millionaire vlogger Felix Kjellberg, a.k.a. PewDiePie, started with a Shopify store (pewdiepiestore. myshopify.com). It sells hoodies featuring his logo, t-shirts and hats with his favourite sayings, and beach towels and backpacks with his pet pugs on. In the UK, Marcus Butler's shop (marcusbutlershop.com) sells cushions featuring one of his favourite sayings, 'Wake me for food!' alongside hoodies and t-shirts featuring a caricature of Marcus delivering his popular intro, 'Hello!'

What will you sell? Watch some of your old videos to see if there is a catchphrase that you use a lot. Is there a pet or an object that features in lots of your videos? Was there a particular vlog that your audience really loved because of some blip or mistake? What videos, or aspects of your videos, do your audience keep talking about in the comments section?

There's more to merchandise than t-shirts. You can put your logo and catchphrase on anything from USB keys to alarm clocks. If you don't believe your audience would wear t-shirts, then think about things they would actually use – from toothbrushes to handbags. What subjects do you talk about in your videos? What subjects are related to those products that you can put your logo on? By picking products that your viewers will use often, you are increasing your chances of brand exposure to a larger audience. When viewers use your branded merchandise in public, their friends will see it and should start to recognise your logo, hopefully checking out your vlogs for themselves.

You can make branded merchandise with no start-up costs at the websites Spreadshirt (spreadshirt.co.uk) or CaféPress (cafepress.co.uk). These sites allow you to upload your own designs and use them on different products. Spreadshirt is largely clothes- and accessories-focused, but CaféPress has more than 250 items that you can brand with your logo, cartoon or saying.

To get started, simply visit the websites, and click on the tab *Sell* in the header. You'll be asked to apply, which simply means registering your details. Once you have an account, all you need to do is upload your designs and pick which products you want to put them on.

CaféPress lets you customise your own Café Press shop, which is worth doing as it increases brand awareness and makes your viewers feel confident that they're buying genuine products. You can create your own custom header featuring your vlog's logo, and customise the design so it's easy for shoppers to locate the products they want. For example, you might feature best-selling or new products at the top of the shop so they catch a customer's eye. This is the equivalent of shops having large in-store displays to make sure shoppers see certain promotions.

Once you've set up your store, you're responsible for promoting it. You wouldn't make a video and hope people would find it on YouTube, would you? No, you'd spread the word on social networks and tell as many people as you could. That's what you need to do for your online shop. Post photos on Facebook, Twitter, Snapchat and Instagram. If someone else posts a picture of themselves using one of your products, retweet it or repost it on Instagram. Show your viewers you appreciate their custom.

Don't forget the obvious – use your vlog to promote your products. There's a prime opportunity for product placement here. Use a mobile-phone case with your logo on, drink from a branded coffee-cup, wear a t-shirt or have a handbag lying around. Include a call to action in your videos, telling readers how they can buy these products and why they should buy them. Create annotations and cards to pop up when the item is shown on screen. The annotation would explain what the product was and direct people to the store, so you could say something like: 'You can buy a mug like mine here'. Then you would set the annotation or card to link directly to the URL of your online store.

Here's a list of successful vloggers who sell merchandise. Before you start your own product line, get some inspiration by looking at what their online stores sell.

- Caspar Lee – Casparleeclothing.com
- Alfie Deyes, PointlessBlog – Pointlessblogshop.com
- Charlie McDonnell, Charlieissocoollike – store.dftba.com/collections/charlie-mcdonnell
- Dan Howell, Danisnotonfire, and Phil Lester, AmazingPhil – danandphilshop.com/
- Troye Sivan – store.troyesivan.com
- KSI – sidemenclothing.com

BOOKS

Once you have a loyal audience who regularly watch your videos, there's a high chance they'll buy a book written by you. When people like hanging out with you online, it's only a small step to persuade them to hang out offline with you. Audiences like books because they can consume all the content in one sitting or space it out over the course of a few nights, and re-read it as many times as they want.

Many of the world's best-known vloggers have written books, and these have been so successful that they've smashed book sales figures. The most famous example is Zoe Sugg's book, *Girl Online*, which sold 78,109 copies in its first week of release in November 2014. No other author since 1998, when Nielsen started compiling its BookScan sales figures, has ever achieved this many sales with their debut novel. By comparison, *Fifty Shades of Grey* by E.L. James sold 14,184 copies in its first week, and Stephanie Meyer's

Twilight sold just 53. Those titles sold more over time through word of mouth, but so did Zoe's. The difference was that she had 6 million subscribers when she released her book, and her pre-existing fan base snapped up her work.

Zoe's boyfriend Alfie Deyes released his first book, called *The Pointless Book*, in September 2014. In its first week of sales it shifted 15,330 copies – more than any other book at that time, bearing in mind this was before his girlfriend's record-breaking achievement. The book shot straight to the top of both the Amazon and *Sunday Times* bestseller lists and has now sold over 150,000 copies, prompting a second book, *The Pointless Book 2*. However, what really shocked publishers when Alfie's book was released was the number of people who turned up to his first-ever book-signing. Normally an author is lucky to attract a hundred or so people, but more than 8,000 people showed up to see Alfie at Waterstone's in London's Piccadilly Circus, causing police to arrive and close down the store.

Other vloggers-turned-authors include Michelle Phan with *Make Up Your Life: Your Guide to Beauty, Style and Success – Online and Off*, Grace Helbig with *Grace's Guide: The Art of Pretending to Be a Grown-Up* and *Grace & Style*, Tanya Burr with *Love, Tanya*, Dan Howell and Phil Lester with *The Amazing Book is Not on Fire*, Joe Sugg with the graphic novel *Username: Evie*, Joey Graceffa with *In Real Life: My Journey To A Pixelated World*, PewDiePie with *This Book Loves You* and Olajide 'KSI' Olatunji with *KSI: I Am a Bellend*.

Look at these books and you'll find they're all very different. Zoe and Joe Sugg have created works of fiction, whereas Tanya

Burr and Alfie Deyes have centred their books on the content of their videos, writing about beauty and silly things respectively. PewDiePie and KSI focus on comedy, with their books uplifting readers and leaving them feeling just as happy as their videos do. Therefore there are no hard-and-fast rules when it comes to choosing what to write about.

If you'd like to write a book, the most important thing is to be passionate about your subject. Zoe Sugg has said she always wanted to write fiction, and her brother Joe has spoken about his love of graphic novels. Other vloggers might not have these ambitions, and are more passionate about the subjects they cover in their vlogs. You must ask yourself – what am I so interested in, that I could write over 80,000 words about that subject? The writing process is not easy and requires a lot of alone time, and if you're not truly interested in your subject you'll want to give up after a few writing sessions. Don't pick a book subject by thinking about what others would like to read or by looking at what type of book has done well. The most important thing is that you're interested in it, so that you finish it. Sales will come if you can demonstrate to your vlog viewers that you are passionate about your work. Enthusiasm is contagious!

Once you've chosen a topic, you have two options – persuading a traditional publishing house to offer you a deal, or self-publishing.

The publishing house route depends largely on your figures. Publishing houses, just like shops stocking beauty products, don't like to take risks. They are responsible for the print runs and costs involving staff to edit and promote the book. If your average views per video and subscriber numbers aren't high enough, there's little chance they'll sign you, no matter how good your idea is. Don't bother approaching publishers unless you have more than a few hundred thousand subscribers, or you can demonstrate to them how you will grow your channel with planned upcoming collaborations.

If you feel confident about the size of your audience, then you want to persuade a publisher like Keywords Press to take you on. In November 2014, Simon & Schuster's Atria publishing group teamed up with United Talent Agency to launch Keywords Press, which was billed as an imprint devoted to giving 'digital innovators' (i.e. vloggers) a platform from which to build upon the success they've garnered online. 'We're trying to approach everything that we're doing from a different point of view and a different perspective, which is why we want a whole imprint as opposed to reaching out to individual authors,' said Judith Curr, President and Publisher of Atria and Keywords Press. '[Our authors] don't come to us with a fully-formed proposal. Rather, we're working with them and their team on what it is they're really passionate about and really committed to, and then we work from that perspective. We're not just translating YouTube content into books.' Keywords Press aims to publish six to ten titles per year, from fiction and nonfiction to offbeat memoirs for adults and picture books for kids. Zoella's book *Girl Online* was their first release and famously broke all sales-figure records.

Most publishers won't read unsolicited manuscripts, so the way to approach them is through a literary agent. Use the *Writers' & Artists' Yearbook* or do a Google search for 'literary agents'. Agencies' websites will explain how to submit proposals to them, but as a rule they require an author bio, a synopsis and a chapter plan. Some also require the first three chapters of a novel. This will test whether you're truly passionate about the subject of your book.

Self-publishing, on the other hand, is not reliant on vlog views or subscriptions, and you can control how quickly you write it and how quickly it's published. Whereas traditional publishing houses take from six months to a year to publish a book, you can write and self-publish a book in as little as two months (although it's not advisable to rush it and make mistakes).

There are many benefits to self-publishing. Create a book that sells well and you may find you make more money from book sales than YouTube advertising. When you self-publish, you get to keep more of the profits. With a traditional publishing house, you may make about 8 per cent of the cover price of paperback sales, but you will make about 70 per cent of the cover price of e-book sales if you charge £1.99 or more on Amazon using Kindle Direct Publishing. It all adds up!

It's not unusual for people thinking of self-publishing to feel a bit ashamed, as if their book isn't 'good enough' for traditional publishers. That's not the case any more, as the number of self-published authors is rapidly growing. In 2014, traditionally published e-books made up only 55 per cent of all Kindle e-books sold on Amazon, with the other 45 per cent being self-published e-books, according to Nielsen PubTrack's e-book statistics. Also, let's not forget that some of the most successful authors in history self-published. Jane Austen self-published *Sense and Sensibility*, borrowing money from her brother Henry to pay a publisher to print the work; she ended up recouping a profit. Laurence Sterne self-published *The Life and Opinions of Tristram Shandy*, which is now considered to be a literary classic, but no traditional publisher would accept it in the 1750s.

Amazon's Kindle Direct Publishing has been around since August 2012 and is a relatively easy way to start self-publishing. As it's owned by Amazon, finished e-books are uploaded directly to Amazon's sales platform and available to the hundreds of thousands of people who visit Amazon daily. The best news of all is that there are no start-up costs.

Visit the Kindle Direct Publishing website (kdp.amazon.com) and sign up for an account. It will talk you through the process of formatting, uploading and publishing your book. Formatting is very important as nothing puts readers off faster than a book that looks unprofessional. Fortunately, Kindle Direct Publishing allows you to write your document using your own software, such as Microsoft Word, and then convert it into Kindle format. To make sure there are no nasty surprises upon conversion, it's advisable to make use of all the information in the Help section of the Kindle Direct Publishing website (kdp.amazon.com/help). Once you're on the Help page, you can access a formatting guide. Look for the Publishing Process section in the left sidebar and then the Before You Start Publishing link. Then click on *Building Your Book for Kindle*, which will bring up the guide explaining page breaks, indentations and fonts.

You'll be asked to upload a cover for your e-book, and it's worth taking time over the design as, sadly, people do judge books by their covers. The Kindle Direct Publishing website has a tool to help you design your own cover art, but, unless you are particularly skilled in this area, you should delegate. Visit Fiverr (fiverr.com), where freelancers sell services for just five dollars, and you'll see many Kindle e-book design pitches. Enter 'Kindle cover' in Fiverr's search box and take your pick.

Next you'll be asked to set copyright details. Amazon will ask if you are marketing the book as a public domain title or if you own the copyright. You own the copyright if the book is your own work, so you should tick this box and also tick *Worldwide distribution*. After all, you want to reach as many people as you can, don't you?

Pricing is the difficult step. Self-publishing allows you to work out what you want to charge for the book. When you search Google for 'Kindle pricing strategy', you'll see there are masses of surveys and studies about how different prices mean different sales. One school of thought is that a 99p e-book is powerful as you can sell tens or hundreds of thousands of copies at this price. However, this strategy works best for completely unknown authors. You're not completely unknown as people know you from your vlogs, so you can get away with setting the price higher.

Studies have shown there seems to be a sweet spot of £2.99, a price that readers are prepared to risk on a self-published author. When you set your price higher than 99p, it shows you have confidence in your writing ability and faith in your brand, and readers will be inspired by that. They think they'll be getting something special for a £2.99 e-book. Also, if you're an established vlogger and you price your book at 99p, people will wonder what's wrong with it. It could harm your vlog traffic if you price your book too low, as viewers will assume it's poor quality. Then they'll start to question the quality of your videos.

Kindle Direct Publishing works only with e-books, so, if you want to sell physical copies, you'll need another publishing platform. The easiest way to do this is with a print-on-demand service, which means there are no upfront costs: books are printed only when your customers order them.

Before you jump into this, ask yourself whether your audience has a big appetite for a physical book. Physical copies are great for vloggers who spend a lot of time out and about, giving speeches or hosting events, as they can set up a stall to sell their books at a venue. But what about if you – and your audience – spend most of your time online? Kindle can be accessed by anyone with a smartphone and a Kindle app, so if someone can watch your videos there's a high chance they'll be able to consume your Kindle e-book. You might be better off spending time promoting an e-book than registering with a print-on-demand service and uploading your manuscript.

If you do get out and about a lot and want to thrust physical copies of your book into people's hands, the most popular print-on-demand service is CreateSpace (createspace.com), which is also operated by Amazon. Again, there are next to no start-up costs, and your book is made available on Amazon.com. In return, Amazon deducts 40 per cent of the retail price, giving you a 60 per cent royalty. You are also provided with your own CreateSpace e-store where your sales earn 80 per cent royalties. The book will also be available on Amazon.co.uk and Amazon

Europe, but the amount of commission you earn varies outside of the US. The CreateSpace website has a tool that allows you to calculate commission, based on the price you'll sell your book for and the number of pages it has.

Other advantages of CreateSpace are free Word templates for formatting your book's interior. The templates come in a wide range of sizes to match the most common print book sizes. In addition, they offer step-by-step instructions on how to convert your formatted file to PDF ready for upload. Usefully, there is a free interior reviewer tool where you can upload and check your Word or PDF interior file before you order your hard copy preview. There is no charge if you need to make proofing corrections and re-upload your file, provided the page count stays the same.

The only charge you should pay is a postage fee to order your initial proof copy. CreateSpace does try to sell you some extra services such as Extended Distribution, which means your book will be made available to the large US wholesalers and in turn included on data feeds that go out to the main US bookstores and US online retailers. However, for UK publishers this is not worth the cost. Royalty rates are much lower and your main customers will be in the UK anyway. Even if you're based in the US, the cost is not worth it as store owners will see that the book is published by CreateSpace and fulfilled by Amazon, and will be less inclined to take it on. If you want to see your book in a store, the best option would be to use another print-on-demand service so the ISBN (Individual Standard Book Number) of your book can't be traced back to Amazon. But as you're a vlogger, most of your audience spend a large proportion of their time online and are more likely to shop at Amazon than visit a physical store. Don't let the hassle of high-street stockists' ISBNs confuse you – just don't sign up for any extra services except a proof copy of your work.

Once you're happy with the proof, you can order author copies at a discounted rate which you can take to events, parties and trade shows and sell for a higher price. Remember to take a large poster or sign broadcasting that the books are on sale and some change for people paying with notes.

To give you an idea of how much it's possible to make, imagine you sold 5,000 e-books for £1.99 through Kindle Direct Publishing. You'd make £1.39 on each book, meaning you'd make almost £7,000 in total. Think about all the people you know, all your social media followers and all your vlog viewers. Then think about how many other vloggers you know whom you could persuade to feature news of your book's release. Suddenly, £7,000 seems quite achievable, doesn't it? Sell 10,000 and you're looking at £14,000, which is not bad if the book's based on your vlog's content and took a matter of months to complete. Release a sequel and that's an extra £7,000 to £14,000 on top of the money you make from your vlog in sponsored content and YouTube advertising.

MUSIC

If you've always wanted to belt out a ballad like Mariah Carey, rap like P Diddy or dance like Jennifer Lopez, then music could be a great promotional tool for your vlog and earn you money at the same time. The money you make won't be enough to give up your day job, but it could turn out to be a nice sum in addition to the money you make from your vlog. Successful vloggers make money from multiple revenue streams and, if you're musically inclined, this route is open to you. If you're not musically inclined and you don't mind making a mockery of yourself, this path is still open to you – there's a chance your video could be so bad that it goes viral, as everyone laughs at how silly it is.

Olajide 'KSI' Olatunji is a great example of a vlogger who's used music to boost his profile and income. He does it because he loves creating silly tunes, and you can see he's enjoying himself in each music video he makes. If he was only doing it to make money, it would show in the quality of his music; and it's important that you only go down the music route if you're genuinely interested in songwriting and performing. Do it with the sole purpose of making money and it will backfire, as your song will be a flop, the music video will receive remarkably fewer views than your other vlogs and you won't earn any money – people can see when you're not being genuine!

KSI's most successful single, *Lamborghini*, which he made with rapper P Money, made Number 30 on the UK singles charts. It was released on iTunes for 99p, and, according to the terms of iTunes, an artist usually makes 9p profit on each single downloaded. Top 30 tunes sell on average 10,000 copies, so KSI would have made around £900. You may think that's barely enough to recoup his costs of making the single – and you'd be right – but the video has received more than 30 million views on YouTube, which is a lot more than some of his other uploads. From YouTube advertising on 30 million views, KSI would have made £50,000 to £60,000, which more than covers his costs. He may also have been eligible for royalties from the Performing Rights Society (PRS for Music), which pays a fee to songwriters per YouTube view of their work, provided the songwriter and song are registered with it. The individual fees are tiny (a fraction of a penny), but with enough views they add up. Lastly, KSI's single would have brought him increased exposure because, to get to 30 million views, his audience must have shared the video with their friends, thus introducing KSI to a new group of people who could turn into viewers and subscribers.

KSI has since released more singles, making money with each one. His debut album *Keep Up* was so successful that it was Number 1 in the UK album chart in January 2016, beating Adele and David Bowie.

Not all music releases will be as well-received as KSI's. Thousands of singles are released each week, and they're usually by professional artists who know what they're doing. How are you going to make your release stand out? You can increase your chances of selling copies by examining KSI's game plan closely. His *Lamborghini* rap video was completely insane, featuring him driving the car around London and getting up to mischief. KSI and his friends have tons of energy, making viewers sit up and pay attention. The lyrics of the song are also memorable – while they're just ordinary words, they sound comical as soon as they come out of KSI's mouth. Finally, the video is professionally shot. Three things we can learn from KSI are that successful music videos require an interesting plot, memorable lyrics and a professionally-shot video. Your video must be completely different from anything viewers have seen before or they won't share it. And if they don't share it, you'll barely make enough to recover your costs. Making music is not a guaranteed way of earning money, but it is possible to earn revenue and gain exposure if you have a great idea and a love for a certain genre.

By the end of this chapter, you should have:

☐ Looked at what other vloggers sell in their online shops
☐ Visited the websites CaféPress and Spreadshirt to see what products you can customise
☐ Looked in the *Writers' & Artists' Yearbook* for literary agents
☐ Had a look at the Kindle Direct Publishing website
☐ Visited the CreateSpace website if you'd like to sell physical copies of a book
☐ Watched KSI's music videos and gained an awareness of the elements needed for a successful music video release

CHAPTER 11

INTERNATIONAL COLLABORATIONS AND COMPETITIONS

Have you heard of the saying 'big fish in a small pond'? When you've built up a loyal audience of viewers in one country and are well-known to brands and PR agencies, you're one of the big fish. But there's a whole world out there. It's not enough to focus on finding viewers and brand-collaborators in your own country. To make more money, you will need to expand abroad.

UK-based vloggers have more reason than others to look further afield. The population of the UK is 64 million as of January 2016. Of that, only a small proportion is the age range and sex of your target market. The US, however, has a population of 319 million, and there are 23 million people living in Australia. That's not to mention the United Arab Emirates or Africa. And if you speak a foreign language, more markets open up.

INTERNATIONAL COLLABORATIONS

Most famous UK vloggers have partnered with international stars at some point, and the collaborations have had hundreds of thousands to millions of views. For example, Marcus Butler's video with American Connor Franta, in which they did a British vs American challenge, has received more than 11 million views since they filmed it in 2013. JacksGap's collaboration with US vlogger Tyler Oakley has received 8 million views, and Joe Sugg's video with Tyler has notched up 4 million views. Zoe Sugg has made numerous videos with Grace Helbig from Daily Grace, with more than million views per video.

When securing collaborations, the same rules apply as in Chapter 8. Identify vloggers with similar audiences as yourself and don't try to aim too high. You're more likely to be successful if you approach someone on a similar level to you. Thanks to social media and the YouTube comments box, there's no need to do anything different when asking a vlogger from a different country to collaborate. You don't need to fly around the world and take them for a nice meal. You wouldn't do that even to secure a partnership in this country, for fear you'd look too keen. Simply comment on their videos, interact with them on Facebook, Twitter and Instagram and perhaps give them a shout-out in one of your videos.

But how do you discover influential vloggers who are based abroad? It's so easy to get stuck in a rut with your YouTube viewing habits. When you always watch videos made by vloggers based in your own country, you're not actively looking out for those who are hitting high viewing figures in their domestic market.

Start by doing a Google search followed by a YouTube search. What subject are you making videos about? Which country or countries do you want to aim at? Combine the two by searching 'beauty vlog Australia' or 'cookery vlog Dubai'. Finally, search 'top vloggers' followed by a country to see the most influential vloggers in that territory.

It's also useful to visit the websites of vlogger talent agencies to see who's influential in each country. They list all their vlogging talent on their websites, and, if any vloggers catch your eye, you can take your research further by visiting that vlogger's YouTube channels. Depending on where you're aiming, you could look at:

Australia: Boom Video (boomvideo.com.au)

America: Addition LLC (addition.buzz), Lennon Management (lennonmgmt.com)

Great Britain: Gleam Futures (gleamfutures.com), OP Talent (optalent.com)

Canada: Wanderlust Management (wminfluencers.com)

When you work with vloggers from new markets, you open yourself up to more brand sponsorship. If you've collaborated with an Australian vlogger and an Australian brand wants to grow traffic in your home territory, they're more likely to choose you than a vlogger who has never showed any interest in Australia.

To secure sponsorship from a foreign market, apply similar rules to those outlined in Chapter 9 when identifying and pitching to brands. Identify both regional and national businesses, and don't be disappointed if you're only appealing to smaller companies at the start. Do the little jobs well, cement your reputation for being reliable and professional and more brands will clamour to work with you.

Be aware that some brands will be more interested in collaborating with you than others, depending on whether they need traffic from an international market or not. A local clothes shop that doesn't ship to your country is not interested in appealing to your market, as they won't be able to service your viewers. Similarly, a neighbourhood restaurant needs to attract customers only from its immediate area and has nothing to gain from an international collaboration. Therefore you must brainstorm what foreign products are easily available to buy in the UK and what services started by foreign companies are available to use in the UK. The types of businesses that will benefit most from international collaborations include:

- Hotel chains
- Tourist boards – regional and national
- Airlines
- Online fashion brands with worldwide shipping
- Food and drink brands sold in supermarkets in your country

One of the most different – and difficult – aspects of securing sponsorship from abroad is that you won't be as familiar with the brand's reputation. You can't visit a store or a hotel to see if it fits your brand, so you have to be doubly vigilant with the research you do online. Before you approach a company, you need to do more than look at its website. Do a Google search to find reviews of the company, and a Twitter search to find out what people are saying about the business on social media. It could harm your vlog's traffic if you collaborate with a brand that people don't like.

INTERNATIONAL COMPETITIONS

Another way to reach a new international audience is to enter a worldwide talent-search competition. These are hosted by big brands and by YouTube itself to find a new generation of star vloggers. Often, they're open to entries from around the world to increase the reach of the competition, something that also benefits the brands sponsoring the competition as they gain from increased international exposure. However, some competitions are open only to entries from one territory. These are still worth entering as the brand will always promote the winners and finalists as much as possible, so you will gain more traffic.

YouTube's NextUp is an annual competition that YouTube has organised since 2011 to find talented creators. There are a total of 360 winners chosen from the cities around the world where YouTube has a Creator Space, including New York, Los Angeles, London, Tokyo, São Paulo, Berlin, Paris, Toronto and Mumbai. Winners receive funding, training and mentoring. The 2016 winners received a £1,750 voucher for production equipment, a spot at a week-long creator camp at one of the YouTube Spaces to learn new production and audience-building techniques, and mentoring from previous NextUp graduates.

To submit an application in future, keep an eye out on the YouTube NextUp website (youtube.com/yt/space/events-nextup.html) at the start of the year, as the competition usually opens in January or February. You'll need to respond to three short essay questions about why you want to participate, how you plan to develop your channel over the next year and how you would collaborate with other participants in the programme. You must also submit a YouTube video of no longer than five minutes that represents your channel's level of technical ability, originality and storytelling techniques. In order to be eligible, entrants must be YouTube Partners with between 10,000 and 100,000 subscribers. Accounts must be in good standing with no strikes for misuse of advertising or copyright, and users should have uploaded three videos within ninety days prior to the start of the contest.

CASE STUDY: INGRID NILSEN, A.K.A. MISSGLAMORAZZI

Ingrid was one of the first winners of the YouTube NextUp competition in 2011. Thanks to the push the competition gave her, she reached almost million subscribers by 2016 and has more than a million followers on both Twitter and Instagram. Career highlights include interviewing US President Barack Obama, appearing as a judge on *Project Runway: Threads* and becoming CoverGirl's first YouTube brand ambassador. A video she made where she came out as gay has had more than 13 million views.

Ingrid's advice for vloggers starting out is: 'Go for it! The only thing that's stopping you is yourself,' she said to *New Media Rockstars*. 'I've really come to learn what that saying means now that I'm a YouTuber because I used to hear people say that all the time, and I'd be like, "Okay, whatever", but now I really understand that because there really isn't anything stopping you except your own fears, and I think that if you're afraid you should just go for it.

'Don't worry about what other people are going to think, don't worry about if you're going to get views or not, because you should be doing it because you love it and you're passionate about it. I didn't pay attention to anything for so long; I was just posting videos, I wasn't looking at views or numbers of anything like that, and I think that is the way to go, especially when you're first starting out, because you want to be doing it because you love it, and now I am at a place where I feel so thankful because I love it even more now and I didn't think that was possible.'

'It's hard work. Right now I shoot three days a week,' she told *Stylecaster*, talking about how she grew her channel. 'Shoot days at the least are six hours long, and can go up to twelve hours long. It's a process just shooting the videos, and there's a lot of planning that goes into that. The planning happens before that, so on two separate days of the week I'm usually planning for other videos, answering emails, editing, and doing all of the other stuff. A lot of the time my weeks don't end where the weekends begin. I just try to give myself some time on Sundays to binge-watch Netflix.

'Planning is important. At the beginning of everything, for me, is coming up with a concept. It really starts with the idea, and the products, and the way that it's shot, and all of that comes into play. As for idea inspiration, it's a little bit of everything from everywhere. I listen to what my viewers want, and I get inspiration literally everywhere I am. I'm always taking notes and writing things down. I can be out and pull out my phone for random notes. I have a running list of ideas at all times.'

TIP: SIGN UP FOR A FREE COURSE AT YOUR LOCAL YOUTUBE SPACE

One of the prizes of the NextUp competition is a five-day course for all the winners, where they receive expert advice on technical issues and collaborations. But did you know that YouTube often holds bootcamps about all manner of useful subjects in its local spaces in London, New York and LA?

Courses include Building Your Channel (which covers producing videos on a budget, growing an audience and making money with YouTube), An Introduction To Final Cut Pro X (to improve editing skills) and Camera Buffet (introducing vloggers to different types of cameras including GoPro HERO4, Canon 70D/5D, Canon C100/C300/C500, 4K Blackmagic and Sony FS700).

Get into the habit of regularly checking the website for your local YouTube space, for example youtube.com/yt/space/london.html. You'll see new events pop up all the time. Some events do require a minimum number of subscribers but this could be anything from 500 to 5,000.

The best way to find out about new or upcoming vlogging competitions is regularly to search 'vlog talent search' or 'vlog competition' in Google. Make-up brand Rimmel London hosted a cool competition in December 2015 to find their latest brand ambassador. They invited vloggers from around the world to film tutorials using Rimmel London make-up and upload them to the London Look section of the Rimmel London website. Fifteen finalists from countries around the world – including Argentina, Canada, France, Spain and the UK – were paid to travel to London, to work on a make-up tutorial with Rimmel London's celebrity ambassador Rita Ora and network with each other. The overall winner received a sponsorship deal to be an ambassador for Rimmel London.

One of the biggest competitions recently held in the UK was Vlogstar, hosted by mobile network O_2 and TV channel 4Music. The winner of the competition – Munyaradzi 'Munya' Chawawa – became the face of 4Music online, with a presenting job interviewing bands and providing backstage footage of performances. He also received a Panasonic HD camcorder, a Samsung Galaxy and an O_2 Big Bundles SIM to help produce his vlogs. All he had to do was make a video predicting what he thought would be popular that summer. If you think you can do the same, make sure you search for talent competitions regularly.

By the end of this chapter, you should have:

☐ Made a list of influential vloggers based in foreign countries
☐ Made a list of foreign brands that may want exposure in your market
☐ Bookmarked YouTube's NextUp website so you're aware of upcoming competitions
☐ Searched Google for other vlogging competitions. You have to be in it to win it!

CHAPTER 14

THE FUTURE
OF VLOGGING

Once you start vlogging and making money, you'll have to face a lot of jealous people. These people love to put doubt in your mind and make you question why you're vlogging. They often ask what will happen in ten or twenty years' time. They bring up Myspace, which had six years of explosive growth until it was usurped by Facebook at the start of 2009, and question whether YouTube will suffer a similar demise. Or they ask about what a beauty vlogger will talk about when she's fifty or sixty years old. Neither of these weak arguments should concern you. If you want to get started in vlogging or build up your channel, then go ahead! Online video is not likely to shrivel up and die any time soon.

There are two reasons why vlogging looks set to survive – and thrive – as a form of content creation and consumption.

Firstly, companies like YouTube are constantly adapting their technologies to provide vlog and online video viewers a better experience. As they're moving with the times, they're always adapting to the tastes and preferences of a new generation, unlike now-defunct platforms like Myspace which never pioneered new technology. Secondly, a vlogger's audience tends to be loyal. Once a vlogger has earned the respect of viewers and subscribers, their audience will support them and grow with them. As long as a vlogger can maintain an audience by interacting with viewers and making them feel valued, they can monetise the audience online and offline, even if the content they're producing has massively changed from when they first started out.

Let's look at each point in more detail:

TECHNOLOGY

With the rise in popularity of online video, more companies are trying to get in on the act – from Facebook video and Snapchat to Vimeo and Vessel. This is a great thing for vloggers, as all these companies are competing among themselves to give viewers and video-makers the best possible service. In conference rooms at these companies' head offices, developers are thinking up ways to make it easier for people to consume video and to make the experience more entertaining. This helps keep vlogging fresh and relevant, and vloggers themselves don't have to do anything but keep producing content.

YouTube is leading the way with a big push towards virtual reality. They've developed Google Cardboard, which is a DIY kit to make a virtual-reality headset from a piece of cardboard. A smartphone neatly slots inside the headset once it's assembled to immerse a viewer into the content.

Robert Kyncl, YouTube's Chief Business Officer, told the 2016 Consumer Electrics Show (CES) conference: 'Digital video can provide a much more immersive and interactive experience than TV. On YouTube, we made an early bet on 360-degree 3D Video, because this is the first type of video that gives you a better experience on mobile than on desktop and TV. Since we know that mobile is expanding, formats that lend themselves to mobile storytelling will grow alongside them quite rapidly.

'We've partnered with GoPro to create the first 360-degree 3D camera on the market, called the Odyssey. Odyssey uses sixteen GoPro cameras to create Virtual Reality video and automatically stitches it together using Google's Jump technology. We're putting VR cameras in our YouTube spaces around the world and working with leading partners to encourage creators to tell richer, more interactive and more immersive stories. We've democratised the most intimidating part of the VR experience – viewing – by creating Google Cardboard. For just a couple of dollars, anyone can have access to a completely immersive experience that works with any smartphone.

'The place for all that to live is YouTube. Already on Android, and soon on iOS, you'll be able to watch any YouTube video in VR using Cardboard, making VR truly democratic and prime to grow exponentially.'

Another way YouTube plans to shape the future of online video is with its Google Red subscription service. Launched in the US in October 2015, subscribers pay $9.99 a month to access ad-free videos and premium content, and gain the ability to cache media for offline viewing. Upon its launch, some media commentators called it a rival to Netflix, but the only similarity with Netflix is the subscription-service model. YouTube doesn't have the licences for TV shows from major networks or movies from major studios, nor does it seem interested in acquiring them. Instead, the YouTube Red original content will come from the online video industry's creative community, so it's more accurate to think of the new service as a way for YouTube to upsell its most dedicated users by promising them an exclusive-content tier.

Viewers benefit from YouTube Red as they get to see original content from their favourite vloggers like PewDiePie and Joey Graceffa that they wouldn't see without a subscription. Vloggers benefit as YouTube shares the subscription revenue with the video-makers that people are watching. With the introduction of more ad-blockers, vloggers' advertising revenue from YouTube has taken a dip in recent times, and this is a way they can earn more cash without having to make changes to their format.

Vlogger Hank Green posted in October 2015 a recent video discussing YouTube Red. He considers a hypothetical YouTube super-user who watches two hours of video on the site each day. Given the current state of YouTube ad rates, that user will generate only about two or three dollars in revenue each month. If that user signs up for YouTube Red, however, he generates $9.99 per month. And since YouTube's Robert Kyncl has stated that YouTube is sharing the 'vast majority' of its subscription revenue with creators, YouTube Red has the potential to make creators a lot more money than they could ever make from ads.

There are plans to roll out YouTube Red around the world, and YouTube has made significant progress on a UK launch by extending its licence with PRS for Music. PRS for Music represents the rights of 115,000 songwriters, and YouTube's Head of Music, Christophe Muller, told *Music Business Week* magazine: 'We're committed to ensuring that writers, composers and publishers continue to get paid and that our users have the best experiences enjoying the video content that they love. This deal is an important step in delivering both of these priorities and speaks to a bright future ahead. 2016 will see yet more opportunities for creators, authors and composers as we launch new products and create new revenue streams.'

YouTube is doing the hard work of developing new products and securing licences to remain relevant in the future. This means vloggers can continue to do what they're doing, and the money will keep coming in.

AUDIENCE GROWTH

Vlogging builds friendships. When viewers watch a vlog, they're interacting with the vlogger as a friend. They leave comments in the comments box and like the videos, and this influences the way a vlogger makes videos in future. As vloggers change their content in reaction to comments, the viewers feel like they're being understood and that they matter, so they're more likely to continue watching that vlogger's work. It's not the same as watching a TV show, in which different characters come and go, and the viewers have no say on the direction of the programme. When a TV programme stops being relevant to a viewer's life, they'll switch off straight away. If a vlog starts to become less relevant, viewers will stick with it for longer and give the vlogger feedback before they give up.

Viewers of vlogs are less likely to feel the need to move on. Viewing habits do change as people age, and someone who liked watching soaps on TV in their twenties and thirties may move on to documentaries in their forties and fifties. In the same way, someone who liked watching beauty videos in their teens and twenties may want to watch content about more serious subjects like raising children or careers as they hit their thirties. But don't forget that vloggers age too. The person who vlogged about beauty as a youngster may want to cover other subjects as they grow older, and it's possible for vloggers and their viewers to grow and change simultaneously.

Dominic Smales, founder of vlogging talent agency Gleam Futures, believes:

'Digital talent will always be important to audiences – now and in the future. Viewers are consuming more and more content online. They're not going to go backwards as they get older and revert back to TV. They'll grow as the vloggers grow.

'The content vloggers make may end up on more platforms, but the audience will remain loyal to the talent. This is because vloggers are able to have a direct relationship with their audience. They have the flexibility to make the content they want and that their viewers want. They don't have to persuade any commissioners to make a programme, and there are no gatekeepers standing in the way between vloggers and their viewers. If a vlogger wants to go in a different direction, they can, and if their audience is loyal they'll move with them.'

The vlogger Estée Lalonde, who used to vlog under the name Essie Button, is evidence of how vloggers can rebrand over time and grow with their audience. When she started out in 2010, she posted mainly about beauty, covering everything from make-up hauls to her skincare routine. However, as she has grown up, her interests have evolved – so she reflected that in her rebrand of 2015. Now she posts about every aspect of her life – not just beauty – and says that using her real name Estée Lalonde, as opposed to Essie Button, makes everything feel more personal and gives her more creative scope.

In a video announcing the rebrand, she said: 'I just hope people see me for who I really am. I'm a twenty-five-year-old woman who's created her own career, who lives with her boyfriend and we have a house and a dog together – I'm a grown-up. I hope people just see me as more of a woman now.' Her advice for up-and-coming vloggers is similar – be yourself and your audience will come. She added: 'I think it's important to just focus on coming across as who you really are, because at the end of the day it's personality and the content that's really going to matter. Just get started.'

Has it worked for Estée? The statistics speak for themselves. She has more than a million subscribers, so her audience has not only stayed with her but she's also found new viewers. This could be because she's happier making a new type of content and her passion comes across in her videos.

Vlogger Alfie Deyes is also confident that vloggers will have long-lasting careers. In the BBC show *The Rise of the Superstar Vloggers*, he explained that he's witnessed the industry change since he started out. At the start, everything was done online – from making money to interacting with fans. Now he's done projects offline and his fans have both followed and supported him. He says: 'I think vlogging will grow and grow. It's not just about videos any more. People are buying our books and they're turning up to our meet-and-greets to see us.'

As long as you love what you do, you'll have a future as a vlogger. This is most likely to be on YouTube as long as they keep developing new technologies, but there's nothing to fear if a new mode of content consumption becomes more popular. Simply move with the times and join the new platform, and if your audience likes what you do they'll move with you. Be prepared to be flexible but never compromise who you are or what you believe in.

It might take a while to 'get rich vlogging', but you stand a better chance of it if you focus on content rather than finances. Think about what you can do to get more traffic and more people regularly tuning in to watch your videos, not what you can do to make money in the short term. After following the steps outlined in the chapters of this book, you will have worked out your identity and learned how to alert people to your vlog's existence. The more people you reach, the more money you'll make. Good luck!

KEY PLAYERS GLOSSARY

A TO Z OF INFLUENTIAL VLOGGERS

AmazingPhil by Phil Lester (youtube.com/AmazingPhil) –
3.4 million subscribers

Caspar Lee (youtube.com/dicasp) – 5.9 million subscribers

Catrific by Cat Valdes (youtube.com/catrific) – 730,000
subscribers

Charlieissocoollike by Charlie McDonnell (youtube.com/
charlieissocoollike) – 2.4 million subscribers

Danisnotonfire by Dan Howell (youtube.com/danisnotonfire) –
5.6 million subscribers

Estée Lalonde (youtube.com/essiebutton) – 1.1 million
subscribers

Fleur De Force (youtube.com/FleurDeForce) – 1.4 million
subscribers

Key Players Glossary

JacksGap (youtube.com/JacksGap) – 4.2 million subscribers

Jenna Marbles (youtube.com/JennaMarbles) – 15.9 million subscribers

Jim Chapman (youtube.com/jimchapman) – 2.5 million subscribers

Joey Graceffa (youtube.com/joeygraceffa) – 6 million subscribers

KSI (youtube.com/KSI) – 12.8 million subscribers

iJustine (youtube.com/ijustine) – 2.8 million subscribers

Marcus Butler (youtube.com/MarcusButler) – 4.3 million subscribers

Michelle Phan (youtube.com/MichellePhan) – 8.4 million subscribers

Niomi Smart (youtube.com/niomismart) – 1.6 million subscribers

PewDiePie (youtube.com/PewDiePie) – 44 million subscribers

PointlessBlog by Alfie Deyes (youtube.com/PointlessBlog) – 5 million subscribers

Sprinkle of Glitter by Louise Pentland (youtube.com/Sprinkleofglitter) – 2.4 million subscribers

IISuperwomanII by Lilly Singh (youtube.com/IISuperwomanII) – 8.6 million subscribers

Tanya Burr (youtube.com/tanyaburr) – 3.4 million subscribers

ThatcherJoe (youtube.com/ThatcherJoe) – 6.6 million subscribers

Troye Sivan (youtube.com/TroyeSivan) – 4 million subscribers

Tyler Oakley (youtube.com/tyleroakley) – 8 million subscribers

Zoella by Zoe Sugg (youtube.com/zoella) – 10.2 million subscribers

A TO Z OF TALENT AGENCIES

Addition LLP (addition.buzz)

Boom Video (boomvideo.com.au)

Gleam Futures (gleamfutures.com)

Lennon Management (lennonmgmt.com)

Mode Media (thecorp.mode.com/join-us/)

OP Talent (optalent.com)

The & Collective by The & Partnership (theandpartnership.com)

Wanderlust Management (wminfluencers.com)